# Second Chances

# Second Chances

## Top Executives Share
## Their Stories of
## Addiction and Recovery

GARY STROMBERG AND JANE MERRILL

New York  Chicago  San Francisco  Lisbon  London  Madrid  Mexico City
Milan  New Delhi  San Juan  Seoul  Singapore  Sydney  Toronto

**Library of Congress Cataloging-in-Publication Data**

Stromberg, Gary, 1942–
    Second chances : top executives share their stories of addiction and recovery / by
Gary Stromberg and Jane Merrill. — 1st ed.
      p.   cm.
    ISBN 978-0-07-159162-1 (alk. paper)
    1. Executives—Biography.    2. Drug addiction.    3. Drug addiction—Treatment.
I. Merrill, Jane.    II. Title.

HF5549.S77    2009
362.29092'2—dc22                  2008044439

1 2 3 4 5 6 7 8 9 10 11 12 13 14 15 16 17 18 19 20 21 22   FGR/FGR   0 9

ISBN   978-0-07-159162-1
MHID     0-07-159162-1

Page 27: Four lines from "The Envoy of Mr. Cognito," pp. 333–334, used as epigraph,
from *The Collected Poems: 1956–1998* by Zbigniew Herbert. Translated and edited by
Alissa Valles. Copyright © 2007 the Estate of Zbigniew Herbert. Translation copyright ©
2007 by Alissa Valles. Introduction copyright © 2007 by Adam Zagajewski. Reprinted by
permission of HarperCollins Publishers. With additional translations by Czeslaw Milosz
and Peter Dale Scott.

Page 83: The excerpt from the poem "Four in the Morning" by Szymborska, Wislawa,
Krynski, Magnus J. (trans), in *Sounds, Feelings, Thoughts.* © 1981 by Princeton University
Press. Reprinted by permission of Princeton University Press.

Page 133: Five lines from "A Man in His Life," p. 351, used as epigraph, from *Yehuda
Amichai: A Life of Poetry: 1948–1994* by Yehuda Amichai. Translated by Benjamin and
Barbara Harshav. Copyright © 1994 by HarperCollins Publishers Inc. Hebrew-language
version copyright © 1994 by Yehuda Amichai. Reprinted with permission of HarperCollins
Publishers.

Page 201: The excerpt from the poem "Carmel Point," copyright 1954 by Robinson Jeffers,
from *Selected Poetry of Robinson Jeffers* by Robinson Jeffers. Used by permisson of
Random House, Inc.

*To Laurie Filstrip and Marvin Worth*

# Contents

# Foreword

Oone of the first instances of reverence I saw around me as a child was the reverence that my parents had for the moment in the evening when drinking was permitted. They were more reverent about that, about cocktail hour, than they were about church or marriage or even family.

I wouldn't have said my parents' crowd back in the Connecticut suburbs in the sixties and seventies, any more than the work or home settings of the people whose stories you'll read in this book, was virulent, malicious, or even self-serving. I think my parents were just naive. They didn't think ahead about where all the drinking and sleeping around was going to lead. American culture, taken as a whole, was pretty supportive of this approach: having three-martini lunches, smoking pot at parties, sleeping with the secretary, and so forth. I think my parents got married very young, as people did in the fifties, started having children very young (my mother had three kids by the time she was twenty-four), and were then ill-equipped to face their own ambivalences. The drink was at hand thereafter, as it had always been.

I don't think that John Cheever's suburbs of distracted young people and melancholy but well-heeled parents exist anymore in the way they did. I suspect I saw, and perhaps preserved in *The Ice Storm*, the tail end of them. If the suburbs are not significantly less ethnically homogenous now (not in Fairfield County, where I grew up, anyway), the people who live there are at least more tolerant and more aware, ruefully, of the high cost of their ethno-centricity. I don't think the suburbs of the fifties and sixties could happen in the Northeast again. But that doesn't mean that some of the tendencies of that time—the excesses of drink or related problems—don't still afflict families. Those problems are peren-nial. They just get worked out in historically distinct ways.

Are the Svengalis of the business world particularly prone to addiction? I do not think worldly ambition, achievement, and competition automatically entail substance abuse. I suppose I incline toward the view that substance abuse is a mental illness. Not a moral problem, or a by-product of environmental stresses, but a mental illness. And I would probably argue that most if not all mental illness is somatic in origin, whether by reason of genetic predisposition or by reason of bad chemistry. Somatic origins are, at least, co-factors. So I believe substance abuse is not a choice and that environmental factors hasten or help to bring about what is likely a destiny in any event. I for one felt like I had a sub-stance abuse problem long before I had any of the substances in my bloodstream.

This is not to say that my own mixture of character issues did not in some way make substance abuse comfortable or inevitable. And it's perhaps true that my life in some rather elite schools and professions was not high-wire enough—was not too demanding, stressful, or overwhelming—to make anyone crazy. But the long and short of it is that I can't and won't blame my circumstances for what happened to me. I'm the one who opened all the bottles and called the dealer for the drugs. Not everyone in my circle did that. But I did. So the problem was in me. And probably still is, despite the fact that it's been a long while since I did any drinking or took any drugs.

I'm no sociologist, so I don't have facts at my fingertips and have nothing more to offer than anecdotal information—my experiences and those of others around me. But I never associated addiction with status. It has always seemed to invite the rich and poor alike. One man's coke spoon is another man's crack pipe. I have noticed, perhaps, that the children of my close friends are appropriately leery of harder drugs, which is in their favor. But they are just as fond of drinking and smoking pot as kids were in my day. And you can do plenty of damage with these things. I do worry about the crystal meth scourge and the way that this drug has really ruined some less advantaged towns in the middle of the country. Still, it's hard not to conclude that self-destruction will always be there—because it's inborn, because it's a mental illness—and will always grab whatever, whoever is at hand. I wish it weren't so. I hope that there are more treatment options and better education about getting sober than were available twenty or thirty years ago.

Addicts caught in the early phases of the disease would have to know and admit to themselves what they are doing in order for any reasonable conversation to take place. If an addict is admitting, then he or she is on pretty solid footing, because the first important step toward getting clean is this: you have to be honest about what you're up to. Even when I have known people who were bent on continuing drinking, or using, or gambling, or what have you, I have felt that there was reason to hope if they had the capacity to be honest. The disease of addiction, by and large, has dissembling built into it. Or, at least, that's my experience. And it's only when you begin to tell the truth that you start to move in the direction of the light, as it were. Obviously, you want people who are using to be careful and to consider the impact of their addiction, their illness, upon family and friends. Unfortunately, appeals to reason are all but completely worthless in these conversations. Addicts can be way too smart, or too seasoned in the practice of manipulation. The best you can do is to remind this poor fellow: just don't lie to yourself.

A common mistake lies in imagining that with enough willpower one can somehow avoid being an addict. To me, this approach coheres with the tough-love view of the world. I should have, in this view, just been a little stronger, and then I wouldn't have gotten into all this trouble. But I think people who feel this way, who think tough love is a good approach, have never much been addicted, nor do they understand what it feels like inside to be an addict or an alcoholic.

I didn't care about the bad "role models" I saw around me, the wastrels and ne'er-do-wells, because I was only worried about finding a way out of the misery of my own youth. To the extent that I could be unconscious, I felt better. I didn't give a shit about "role models," good or bad, or, at most, I felt that I would worry about them later on. I didn't care if I was hurting myself, because I already hurt a fair amount anyhow. Sometimes I even wanted to be dead. I don't want to overstate the notion, or to make it sound poetical. But that's the truth of the situation. There were many times when I didn't much care if I would make it to age forty. Other addicts of my acquaintance were even less ambivalent. They definitely wanted to be dead. When you think like this, you don't give a shit about role models. You're either drunk, hoping to survive a hangover, or drinking again—or you're doing all of these at the same time.

The addict often habituates, originally, for reasons that are somewhat benign. In my case, I took to alcohol because I was very, very shy as a kid. In the years after my parents divorced, I was uncomfortable. I'd moved around a little bit, changed schools, and I felt that I was scrawny, miserable, easily spooked, not good at sports, unattractive to the opposite sex, et cetera. I was the sort of kid who comes in for a fair amount of torture in most schoolyards. When I first drank with the intent to get drunk, which was in my middle teens, it was a tremendous relief. I felt my phobias and insecurities vanish for the first time. I was confident, comical, and full of enthusiasm—a first! The problem is that you can't, or ought not, rely on a substance for that kind of treatment. The substance, inevitably, will turn on you. As a result, I only got more phobic, more shy, more miserable in the ten years that I continued to drink, drank more, and came to depend on drugs and alcohol to feel that I could function socially in the world. Because there is a fair amount of alcoholism in my family, it was probably predictable that I would develop problems, but I chose to ignore any advice given by responsible adults and to conduct my own experiments. These experiments, as I say, didn't go too well.

Did the worldly successful advantaged types in this book have to go through it? Because I don't think worldly advantaged types have any more luck than street addicts, except that they can afford more in-patient rehab care, I don't think they probably had much choice in the matter. It's best not to romanticize addiction. People are going to try drugs and alcohol, and there is a bit of adventure to it, when you are young and finding your way in the world. But addicts, in the end, are not world explorers. They are people who are poorly equipped for experiment and who therefore settle into addiction like it's a second skin. They find a rut, as the saying goes, and they decorate it. There's no choice involved, after a point—there's only the destiny of doing the same thing over and over and over. This is not romantic. This is pathetic and sad. If *destiny* seems like a large word, it is nevertheless my experience. Whether addiction is truly genetic or whether there are environmental triggers, I am probably not smart enough to say conclusively. But the addict works hard to give up volition, and at least for a time, that's a blessing, because it's precisely the will that is so difficult to operate when you are young and uncertain about life.

I know I do not romanticize the using in my own case. As I have said elsewhere, I was a truly execrable writer as an alcoholic. Mercifully, not very much work from that period remains. I could write at great length on this subject, on the way that alcohol has ruined the arts, and especially the American novel. Addicts, in general, are liars, and even when they are very gifted (William Faulkner, let's say, or Ernest Hemingway), they are liars, and after a point, you can tell in the work. There's an artificial quality to the writing, even when the prose still glitters. My particular problem as an alcoholic writer was that I didn't understand, sympathize with, or care for anyone except myself. Partly, this was protective. I didn't trust anyone—with good reason, it seemed to me. But literature that has only one character is bad literature, and my work was blunted, excessively cerebral, lazy, and sad. It was only in the period of my sobriety that I began to feel something of how other people lived in the world. Now I see this compassionate muscle as one of my strengths. The masses of people, and the majority of writers, even if they are not alcoholics, do prefer the shorthand in which other people are sort of a curse. Dehumanizing is the law of the land. But I feel, in sobriety, a little porous as regards the points of view of my fellow humans. And that makes life and work more interesting. That amounts to a second chance, and it's one I have eagerly taken advantage of.

—Rick Moody

*Rick Moody is the bestselling author of* Garden State *(1992) and* The Ice Storm *(1994), among others. He has also written a memoir,* The Black Veil *(2002). His most recent work is a collection of three novellas entitled* Right Livelihoods *(2007).*

# Preface

As best as I can recall, the ad read, "Wanted. Telephone sales people to earn big commissions working short hours. No experience necessary." It was the last thing in the world I wanted to do, but I needed a job, so I made the call and was instructed to come to an address in an industrial area of Van Nuys, California, a short distance physically but a long ways away from the Hollywood motion picture studios where I formerly reigned as a successful young film producer.

I was new in recovery from years of drug addiction and alcoholism after having blown what was by most standards a pretty decent career in the dog-eat-dog entertainment business. As I've come to accept over the years, I'm what you call a "failed big shot."

So there I was that gloomy morning, reporting for duty in what was known in the business as a telephone boiler room. It was nothing more than a large warehouse filled with temporary cubicles, which contained hard-back chairs on wheels, particleboard desk units, and multiline telephones. Rows and rows of these units created a constant buzz of "super salesmen" laying out their snake oil spiel. I was given a script to read, which was to be repeated word for word on every cold call I made in my attempts to sell large quantities of typewriter ribbons to unsuspecting small business owners. How depressing this all was.

To think that only a year or so before I was riding high as a Hollywood film producer, living large in loopy land. But years of consumption finally caught up with me and destroyed a career I thought was impervious to my indulgences.

Little did I know that my spiral down the drain would lead here. I took this job at the urging of my sponsor in the twelve-step recovery program I was committed to. It was saving my life, and I was willing to do anything he said.

He told me to get working, and, unemployed and desperately low on funds, I did. When I complained that no one would hire me in the film business because of the mess I had made of my life, he pointed out that there were other ways to make a living short of running a film studio. He also suggested that I look for a job that wouldn't require too much time or energy, as I was in good supply of the former but obviously lacking the latter. He wanted me to find a job that I could leave each day without bringing any emotional baggage home with me, so that I could continue to focus on my recovery. He also pointed out that I needed to be self-supporting, which at the time I wasn't. I was living with my parents, in the bedroom I was raised in as a boy. Talk about humiliation.

There is a good side of this story, though, which I need to express here. I was told that if I was willing to do *anything* to support myself and stay with my program of recovery, that sometime in the not too distant future, things would change, and I would find my way back into a successful career. It might not be what I envisioned, but I would be just fine. Well, not long after I signed up for this telephone sales gig, which I should say I was extremely unsuited for (I had the hardest time convincing people they needed to buy lifetime supplies of typewriter ribbon at "huge discounts"), another job was offered to me. One thing led to another, and I was eventually to find my way into a career in public relations, which has sustained me for more than twenty-five years.

Around this time, in my early recovery, I was given a book entitled *A New Pair of Glasses*, by the anonymous author Chuck C, who it turned out was Chuck Chamberlain, the father of actor Richard Chamberlain and a revered member of my twelve-step program. Chuck had been a big-time executive in the supermarket business in southern California, until alcoholism destroyed not only his career but his relationship with his family and friends. He ended up a gutter drunk in Beverly Hills, California.

Chuck explained that when he got sober and worked the program he decided he wanted a career again, but he had a totally different idea on how he was going to go about it. Before he got sober, his work was always about getting ahead and making money. When he found his way into our program and discovered spiritual principles upon which he could build a new life, he made a startling decision for himself. He no longer wanted to work for his own interests, but from now on he would dedicate himself to helping others achieve what it was that *they* wanted to do. "For fun and for free" is how Chuck phrased it. And a surprising thing happened. By being of service to others, Chuck became more successful, by far, than ever before. According to Chuck, money just seemed to flow in when he stopped trying to make it.

It was this remarkable tale that inspired me to get back to work, and to do it for the right reasons. While never able to follow his "for fun and for free" dictum completely, I have, over the years, tried to see how I could be of service to others in my work and not just think selfishly of my own wants and needs. I, too, have found success and, more importantly, peace of mind like I never experienced before.

When it came time to consider another book, after the good response Jane and I had with our first efforts, *The Harder They Fall* and *Feeding the Fame*, I came up with the notion that it would be instructive to do a collective memoir featuring the stories of successful businessmen and -women who lost careers as a result of alcoholism and drug addiction, only to rebuild their lives and careers in recovery.

What follows are the stories of sixteen remarkable people, who share their experiences in hopes that you will be inspired by their examples. I remember thinking when I first started back to work, "I'll never regain what I lost." Well, these people all thought the same thing and are here to tell you that it just isn't so. We hope you enjoy the book, and if you get something out of it, pass it forward.

—Gary Stromberg

# Acknowledgments

We wish to thank the following people for their help in making this book happen:

Randy Spector
Jody Klescewski
Neil Kirk
Mitchell Fink
Dusti Kugler
The Reference Department of the Westport, Connecticut,
  Library

And special thanks to Michel Spitzer for his belief in the project.

# Second Chances

# Michael Deaver

*Change proves true in the day it is finished.*
—*I Ching* (number 49, translated by Thomas Cleary)

Not since Puss in Boots made a king of a drowning miller's son has there been a publicist like Michael Deaver. By all accounts, Deaver revolutionized the face of political image-making, by bringing election campaigning into the TV age.

As President Reagan's media adviser for more than twenty years, Deaver presided over no fewer than eight State of the Union addresses. He held the position of Deputy Chief of Staff from 1981 to 1985. Deaver along with James A. Baker III and Ed Meese were dubbed "the Troika" owing to their impact on policy and over the direction the administration took during their tenure.

He made the cover of *Time* (March 3, 1986) just after he quit as a White House official. That story asked, "What makes Deaver so valuable?" to which it answered, "It is hard to think of a lobbyist who has a better sense of how the Reagan Administration works or who has more clout among the Reaganauts."

Deaver's central innovations came from his belief that most Americans got all their information from television, so, as he told WNYC Radio's "On the Media," "Television was the most important part of my job. . . . I really felt myself more like a producer for television than anything else. Press events were cast consciously to form how the public viewed President Reagan."

As never before, the White House was setting the agenda for the networks instead of the other way around. "The media I've had a lot to do with is lazy," Deaver famously commented. "We fed them and they ate it every day."

A *New York Times* bestselling author, he wrote three memoirs about the Reagans—most notably in 2001, an intimate personal portrait of the president called *A Different Drummer: My Thirty Years with Ronald Reagan.*

Deaver spent his post–White House years as vice chairman of Edelman, a public relations firm with strong ties to the political scene. He was an eminence who advised clients including Republican leaders and heads of major corporations, such as Microsoft, AT&T, Nissan, Fujifilm, Nike, and Kraft, on how to tailor their messages to the media.

His influence moved outside the United States to Asia, Europe, and Latin America. He kept tabs on foreign attitudes toward U.S. business and advised heads of state on how to deal with the Americanized media in their countries. Sadly, Michael Deaver died of pancreatic cancer on August 18, 2007, at age sixty-nine.

That the master of spin dropped the veils to speak of his personal difficulties with alcohol is, we think, remarkable and telling. Deaver embodied everything you'd expect to find from a man in recovery. He was quiet and humble and expressed the gratitude of one whose life was inalterably changed.

---

## MICHAEL DEAVER

I'm the child of alcoholics. Both my mother and father were alcoholics who ultimately stopped drinking but never went into treatment. They stopped drinking in their late seventies and lived into their nineties.

I've always said that alcoholism is the most significant thing about me. I lived with alcoholics, I became an alcoholic—quite an active one—and I've now been in recovery for twenty years. So alcoholism has been the principal factor in all of my life.

When I went off to college, my goal was to never be like my father. I didn't want to drink like him, but by the time I graduated from college, I was a daily drinker, just like he was. It didn't seem to interfere with my life. I wouldn't drink to excess every day; I'd maybe have a couple of beers or a mixed drink, but by and large, very few days went by without me putting alcohol into my system. This went on from the time I was about twenty-one until I was around forty-six or forty-seven. And during that time I had various jobs. I was a piano player for a while, which was not a great occupation for an alcoholic. I was also in politics, which again is not a great place for an alcoholic to be.

I worked on several campaigns, both gubernatorial and presidential. On the various plane flights, when you are traveling with the media on board, there was, of course, a fair amount of drinking going on. We were on very busy schedules, hitting four and five cities a day, maybe six or seven stops in each city, getting on and off of planes. It was hectic.

In my career with Ronald Reagan, I was sort of the number two man, the deputy chief of staff, in the California governor's office and later in the White House when he was president. During the campaigns, I was the manager on the road. I had the responsibility for the candidate, the schedule, the staff, and the speech writing. All of those things came under me in the presidential campaigns of 1976 and then in 1980. In '76, of course, we lost, so I went back to my life in public relations, and Reagan remained a client of mine. It was during this time that I got married and my wife and I had two children.

Usually, I always drank in the evenings. A drink or two, a glass of wine or several. But it never seemed to affect either my career, which was moving along nicely, or my family. I'm sure it did, but I didn't realize it. Then in 1980 I went through another campaign with Reagan, and the big difference this time was that he won the presidency. So my family and I moved to Washington, D.C., and I became the deputy chief of staff of the White House, which was a very serious job.

Though I kept on drinking during this stage of my life, there were days when there just wasn't time for alcohol. I was in my office in the White House by 6:15 A.M. each day, and I didn't get done until at least 7 P.M., six days a week. Maybe on Sunday I'd get to relax a bit, but there was always the White House switchboard to worry about. I could never really escape because my role was so principal to the president and first lady. I was always on call. Even on Sunday there would be five or six calls from either the president or the first lady, or from others in the White House, so I had to keep myself reasonably sober.

But a time came, finally, when I made three or four trips to China, where I was the principal person on the plane. The stewards on Air Force One took very good care of the passengers, and taking very good care of me meant vodka. I came home from those trips and found out I needed a drink at five o'clock in the morning. I had never done that before. My father had done that, and it always bothered me. I always thought, "That was it. If you drank at five o'clock in the morning, you had a serious problem." I rationalized it that very first morning by saying, "Well, you know, it's six o'clock at night in Beijing." So, of course, my body doesn't understand this. And that became the moment when, as I've heard it described, my filter broke. It simply wasn't possible from that moment on to live without alcohol in my system.

I had tremendously high blood pressure in those days, developed from all those years in the White House. The White House doctors put me on beta-blockers. The combination of beta-blockers and alcohol is not good. Even though I was chairman of the second inauguration of the president, I had to leave one of the inaugural activities to be taken to Georgetown University Hospital. One of the doctors there asked me if I could count backward from one hundred. I thought this was a ridiculous question. I think I got to ninety-seven and didn't understand why I couldn't get to ninety-six. I didn't know where ninety-six was.

It turned out that my renal system had shut down because of the combination of beta-blockers and alcohol. When my renal system shut down, my neurological system shut down also, and I became a very sick young man. I was in the hospital for ten days. I decided I had to get out of the White House because I thought the stress of the job was making me so sick. And so I made a decision to leave. When I got out of the hospital, I talked to the Reagans and decided to leave in May of 1985, thinking that this would solve my problem—that not having the weight of the Western world on my shoulders I would now be able to drink.

It didn't quite work out that way. As I continued my drinking, I rationalized it by saying, "It's because I've dedicated my life to public service and I have no money. As soon as I make a million dollars, I'll be able to drink normally." And I did make the money. I made more than that. I had my own PR firm, Michael Deaver and Associates. I was doing very well, and I was still drinking. But there came a time, maybe around 1985 or '86, that I decided I would just like to stay home and drink. It was a Friday, and my wife was away. So I stayed home that Friday and continued drinking on Saturday, Sunday, and Monday. On Monday evening, my then sixteen-year-old daughter came into my bedroom and asked what was wrong with me. I said, "Oh, Amanda, I've got the flu." Beginning to cry, she looked at me and said, "No, you don't. You're an alcoholic." Nobody had ever said that to me, and here was this wonderful child telling me this. So she and I called the doctor and I got into Georgetown University Hospital that night.

The next morning my brother, my business manager, and a couple of doctors were at the foot of my bed telling me I was an alcoholic and I would have to either go to Alcoholics Anonymous or go into treatment, to which I replied, "Well, I can tell you I will never go to Alcoholics Anonymous, so where would you recommend I go into treatment?" They recommended either Hazelden or Father Martin's. I had never heard of either, so I asked where they were. Hazelden is in Minnesota, and Father Martin's was about eighty miles down the road, so I chose the one I thought I could get out of quickly: Father Martin's. That was twenty years ago, and I haven't had a drink since.

I've been on the board of Father Martin's now for over eighteen years. When I got out of treatment, I started going to meetings in a recovery program. Ninety meetings in ninety days. I still go to meetings today. I will go to a meeting tonight. I do a fair amount of work in the field of addiction. October 21, 2006, was my twentieth anniversary of living sober. That is truly a miracle, as we know. Sobriety has changed my life, no question about it.

In 1987, right at the beginning of my recovery, a special prosecutor for conflict-of-interest issues indicted and convicted me on charges of perjury for congressional testimony I had submitted. My life was obviously impacted by this. I lost all of my PR clients. My wife had to go to work. My daughter had just started at Brown University, and my son was in private school here in Washington.

So things were looking pretty bleak. But there was nothing I could do, except go to my recovery group meetings and stay around and close to recovering alcoholics. Of course, they kept telling me that I was getting better, but it was hard to see, as there was nothing getting better around me.

I lost everything. I was sentenced to three years of probation and 1,500 hours of community service, and I was fined $100,000. It just went on and on. Looking back at my trial today, I honestly don't believe I did anything wrong, but the truth of the matter is I probably wouldn't have been indicted if I had been thinking clearly. If I had been sober I would have been able to manage the process better. So I think alcohol had a great deal to do with my problems. Obviously, there were political issues involved, and I was a huge target of the Democrats. I had been Ronald Reagan's closest friend and ally as well as aide for many years. Now I was out on my own and exposed, and I just didn't realize that.

All I had going for me during this time was my family and my sobriety. But I did find myself after a couple of years. I was able to think clearer than I thought I ever would again. There weren't the huge ups and downs in my mental attitude. I was very even, and I was certainly more comfortable with myself than I ever had been up to that point in my life. Because of all the problems I had, I was pretty much ostracized from a lot of what I was used to, even though Reagan was still in office.

It must have been in 1989, after Reagan had left office, when I was in Los Angeles on business and went to a recovery group meeting where they were discussing the making of amends. I had written—but never mailed—letters to Ronald Reagan. I kept showing these letters to my program sponsor, and he kept saying, "These letters are all about you. They need to be about how you affected the other person, not how you were affected." That was some of the best advice I had ever received. So, anyway, after this meeting in L.A., I went back to my hotel and called the Reagans. Nancy answered the phone. I told her that I was in town, that I wanted to see them, but I wanted her to pick a time when I could see both of them together. She said, "Well, how about right now? We're here." I didn't even know where they lived anymore. They had sold the home that I had known in Bel Aire. At any rate, I drove up and found the house. They were very gracious and glad to see me, and I admitted, "There is a real reason for me to be here. I need to tell you both how sorry I am for anything I did to hurt you. In writing my books, or other things that were said that were painful to either of you." They both sat there listening to me and then said, "Don't worry about this; it's not a problem." I was so relieved. As I got ready to leave, we walked to the front door. Suddenly I realized something. Today was Ronald Reagan's birthday. His eightieth, as it turned out. I was so focused on me that I had forgotten. In the past I had never forgotten his birthday, but this day I had.

Reagan, I should tell you, was not a man who ever touched you physically. He was not Bill Clinton, not a hugger, but as I started to leave, he took me in his arms and said, "Mike, this is the best birthday present anyone has ever given me." I don't often tell this story, but it is huge in demonstrating the value of making amends in sobriety.

There was a moment when, as I was driving down the hill from the Reagans' house, I felt like I had removed all the luggage out of my car. And from that day on, my life changed.

I had opened up my own business by that time and I had a few clients. About three weeks after my visit with him, President Reagan called and said, "They're going to dedicate the new Reagan Library. Would you like to run the opening?" It was a public laying on the hands that said I was OK again. Then, after that job was done, I was asked to join the organization I'm still with today, Edelman Public Relations. I was made vice chairman, globally.

Much good has happened. It's been a wonderful, wonderful life. I'm comfortable and I'm respected, but most importantly, I like who I am. My goal today is not getting mentioned in the papers or worrying about what others say about me; my goal today is to put my head down on the pillow at the end of the day and go to sleep.

And to treat everyone fairly. I've had tremendous opportunities open up for me. Not necessarily opportunities for wealth and prestige, but opportunities to help other people. You know that sixteen-year-old daughter I spoke of? Well, she and I have a very special relationship today, as you can imagine. She and her eight-month-old daughter, my granddaughter, live close by. Furthermore, she's in the same business I'm in, and she's very successful and well respected. My son is married, has two children, and lives out in Oregon.

I owe everything to my recovery. The amazing thing about this program I'm in is that I walk into a meeting and I know everything about everyone there, and they know everything about me. When I speak I tell people that I've been in cabinet meetings, National Security Council briefings, meetings with popes, presidents, prime ministers, and kings, but there is nothing more powerful than a room full of alcoholics in recovery. It's the single most powerful thing I've ever experienced.

# 2

# Andrew Zimmern

> *The mind, that ocean where each kind*
> *Does straight its own resemblance find;*
> *Yet it creates, transcending these,*
> *Far other worlds and other seas,*
> *Annihilating all that's made*
> *To a green thought in a green shade.*
>
> —ANDREW MARVELL, "THE GARDEN"

Beloved food expert, chef, dining critic, restaurateur, and media personality Andrew Zimmern is currently best known for his lusty performance on his hugely popular one-hour weekly TV show "Bizarre Foods" on the Travel Channel. This program, which has received unanimous praise from publications including the *New York Times* and *Gourmet* magazine, is an anthropological tour de force featuring "the man with a stomach of steel," the ever-charming, humorous, and culturally sensitive Zimmern.

Born in 1961 and raised in New York City, Zimmern began culinary training at the age of fourteen, apprenticing over the next ten years with some of the world's foremost chefs. Positions as executive chef and general manager for noted New York restaurants followed.

An exceptionally versatile "foodie," Zimmern has written for many national magazines and received the American Society of Professional Journalists Page One Award. He has also lectured on restaurant management and design at the New School for Social Research and consulted in the creation of a number of restaurants.

Eventually he picked up his white toque and moved to new cooking grounds: he, his wife, Rishia, and their son, Noah, have lived in St. Paul, Minnesota, since 1992. There he was executive chef of Café Un Deux Trois for five years, after which he left daily operations to concentrate on his TV career.

Zimmern is also guest chef at many national charity events, food festivals, and galas, and he lectures around the world on cultural culinary matters. In 2002 he was guest of the People's Republic of China, traveling, speaking, and giving demonstrations on Chinese cuisine. Zimmern is truly a world-class entertainment act, an esteemed scholar of food, and an unofficial U.S. ambassador—all in one tasty dish.

---

## ANDREW ZIMMERN

I was born and raised in New York City. My father was an advertising executive, and my mother was a designer. I grew up in the early sixties at a transitional time in America.

My parents were both raised in pretty strict households, and like many other parents during that time, they sort of rebounded completely the other way. So I was brought up in a house that was willing to experiment on how to raise a child, in an era when people were experimenting with all types of lifestyles. We also lived in a home where we really never were wanting for anything. My dad was very high up the food chain in the advertising industry. He, along with a handful of other people, was running what became the third-largest ad agency in the world.

My parents divorced when I was five or so years old. This was the year I tried alcohol, unintentionally. I remember my cousins, at a family Thanksgiving, giving me a glass of champagne, on ice, telling me it was ginger ale. They were all older than me. I drank it. I remember then singing a song, spinning around, and passing out.

I woke up in the car on the way home. Though it wasn't one of those experiences where I felt at one with the world the first time, I do vividly remember saying to myself, "I love this feeling." Even then, I loved what I thought was the glamour of it. I remember, from that moment forward, sipping my dad's drinks when I made them for him. After coming home from the office, he would go and get his mail. It was cute to have his young kid mix him a drink. Even when I didn't mix it, I would steal sips out of it. I remember loving the taste of scotch. I know most young drinkers don't have that experience, but I did.

For the next six or seven years, I was a child of privilege. Although my parents were divorced, I spent a lot of time with them together. More time than when they were married, in fact, because they really made an effort to keep the family together as much as they could.

When I was thirteen, my mom went into the hospital to have an appendix scar covered up with plastic surgery. Bikini lines dropped an inch or two that year. It was 1974, and we had a big house in the Hamptons. She would be on the beach that summer, and she didn't want to have that appendix scar. They gave her the wrong anesthesia during surgery, which cut off the oxygen supply to her brain, and she went into a coma for months and months. I came home from summer camp that year, and my father met me at the airport, which was highly unusual. The limo was there, and we went right to the hospital. My mom was in an oxygen tent, which was a very scary experience for a thirteen-year-old.

I had lived with my mother after my parents were divorced. I remember my father telling me, "We're going to get through this." His mentality was "Let's hold up our heads, keep a stiff upper lip, and get on with our business." He was really solution-oriented, which worked well for him at work but was tough to take as a child. As a parent myself now, I understand what an incredible job he did then, shepherding me through that crisis. He really was doing the best he knew how.

As a thirteen-year-old, I had few tools to handle this tragedy, and the little voice inside my head said, "All right, we won't talk about it." I had teachers, psychologists, my dad, other family members, and friends of our family all spending time with me to give me every opportunity to talk about how I was feeling, but I had no interest in doing that—absolutely none. I thought it was much better to stay silent in order to stop feeling what I was feeling. Somehow, I knew that alcohol could help me with this. And it did. Then friends told me that drugs could do the same thing. I called a friend of mine and asked him if we could go buy some pot. I had only tried it once or twice before. So we went and bought a quarter-pound of grass. We sold a couple of ounces and kept the rest for ourselves. Within a month I was drinking and drugging on a regular basis.

I was thirteen years old, living in my own apartment with a nanny and a nurse. My mother was in a mental institution. My father was still living in his apartment downtown. It was like the movie *Home Alone*. There was a big pile of cash in the hardware drawer in the kitchen. There were charge accounts at the drugstore and the liquor store. Everyone felt sorry for the lonely little rich kid whose mom was in the mental home. I bounced around my friends' homes, staying here and there as I pleased, which was a wonderful experience. I became close with all my friends' parents, but I also had carte blanche to do what I wanted, when I wanted, and how I wanted, and that little frightened child was all of a sudden ruling the roost.

I started fooling around with other drugs, and by the time I graduated high school, I was a daily cocaine user, pill user, pot smoker, and drinker. I got into college, which I chose because it was only two hours away from New York, so I could keep my same drug dealers back home. The ratio at the school was about ten girls to every boy—a real party school. And I made the most of it. I got kicked out during my first year. I spent the first eight out of ten class days attending Grateful Dead concerts at Radio City Music Hall, before getting into my classes. I got out of the dormitory as quickly as I could and moved off-campus to live; I found a situation with older students because I wanted what they had: drugs and booze.

During my freshman year, I developed alcohol poisoning for the first time. I had been drinking nonstop for about thirty-six hours. I woke up in a hospital in Poughkeepsie, New York. The campus police had found drugs on me. D. B. Brown, a drug counselor, did my first intake. He told me I was chronic on the Jellinek Chart (a historic chart that shows the progression of alcoholic decline and recovery), and he said to me, "You know, there is a solution," but I wasn't interested in hearing it. He threw me the life jacket and I tossed it back, because I didn't like the color. I'll never forget the experience of sitting in his office, feeling invincible, and thinking, "I'm too young to be an alcoholic, or a drug addict. I'm only nineteen. I'm strong. I can do this on my own."

I had self-knowledge! I had all these wonderful tools! I was a child of privilege; what rules existed about this condition didn't apply to me because I considered myself to be smarter, faster, and stronger. So much for being smarter: by the time I graduated college, I had a heroin problem as well.

In spite of this, I had also nurtured a love of food and cooking while I was in college. I spent a lot of time cooking in Europe. I spent time cooking in great restaurants in New York and on Long Island during my summers. I loved the food world. It was very exciting being up late. I thought the atmosphere was very glamorous. I never understood why other kids wanted to work for landscape companies during the summer. I wanted to spend my days on the beach with the cute girls and then work at restaurants at night, where all the action was. I was addicted to the action.

I discovered I was talented in the extreme when it came to the food business. So I quickly developed a double life, in which I was hyper-successful: first as a chef, then in the front of the restaurant in New York City, then as the director of a small restaurant group. I encountered and thrived on all kinds of situations in the business. I had the right personality for it. I thought fast on my feet. I understood the front and the back of the house. At the same time, my drug problem was progressing. I was getting bounced out of apartments, I was staying up for three days at a time, I was losing friends. What began as, "Oh, you were so funny last night at that party," quickly turned into, "I can't believe what you did last night. I don't want to go out with you again."

My life quickly turned very dark. I started to get arrested and spent nights in detoxes. I started to be threatened with psych wards by cops who would pick me up on the street. Things turned really bad, really fast. I was kicked out of an apartment that my father had bought for me. Friends wanted nothing to do with me. I burned every bridge. I stole some jewelry and a watch from the mother of one of my friends, hocking them for pennies on the dollar. I eventually ended up homeless, living on the streets. I squatted in an abandoned building on Sullivan Street.

I've walked by that building on Sullivan Street in recovery, with my wife, and told her, "That was the place." Five of us lived in a building with no electricity, cement casements in the windows, and no running water. I didn't bathe for a year. I'd walk on Madison Avenue and steal purses off the backs of chairs in fancy cafés on the Upper East Side. I'd run over to Central Park, vault the wall, catch a train down to the Lower East Side, and sell passports and credit cards from the purses I just stole, to go to my heroin dealers, to support my drinking habit, and also to eat. I was sleeping in this abandoned building every night after I'd pour cans of Comet or Ajax cleaner around the pile of dirty clothes I slept on, so the roaches and rats wouldn't crawl over me in the middle of the night.

I became the guy that people would cross the street to avoid—that crazy, homeless person. Eventually, I went into this hotel that doesn't exist anymore, called the San Pedro. It was sort of a flophouse, but it had a front desk. I checked in with a stolen credit card and gave the guy some money to not send in housekeeping but leave me alone. You know that liquor gets delivered anywhere in the city, so I called and ordered a case of vodka to be delivered to my hotel room, locked the door, and started drinking. That case turned into another case, and another case, and another case. I spent a little over a month in that hotel room, leaving only twice, each time for about an hour. I basically just drank around the clock. I yanked the phone cord out of the wall. I was just trying to drink myself to death. There were winners and losers in life, and there was no point in going on, 'cause I was a loser.

I was petrified of the telephone. I unplugged phones everywhere I was. I didn't want to be contacted. I still struggle with that today, wanting to bury myself in the sand. Especially on the road living this lifestyle. I just want to get away for a day or two. Back then, I loved going off the grid for *months* at a time. No one really wanted to find me anyway. Nowadays, my wife and I sometimes spend thirty-six hours just going off the grid; that feels comfy to me. The change is that now I'm doing it for the right reasons. Just wanting to spend time with my wife and son, getting away from the crazy public life that I lead.

So one morning, I plugged the phone back in the wall, and for the first time in twenty years I did not have that Ace bandage tension around my chest, which I woke up with every morning. The first thing I reached for was a joint or some heroin or a swig of booze. I couldn't start the day straight. I couldn't face the world.

I picked up the phone and called Clark, my best friend from childhood. I said, "Come help me." Right away he said, "Where are you?" So I gave him my address. He came down, paid my bill, got me out of the hotel, and took me to his house. He tried to dry me out. He had one of those boxes under the sink that you would put out if you were having a cocktail party. It contained a bottle of rum, a bottle of gin, a bottle of scotch, and a bottle of tequila. You'd put it out with some mixers. It also had a few bottles of stale wine. Well, within twenty-four hours, I drank everything in that box. Then I stole the change out of the ashtray in his den to go buy more.

Clark sat me down the second day and said, "Andrew, what do you want to do?" I told him that I just wanted some money and to be able to stay for a couple of days. I asked him for a thousand dollars to help me get back on my feet and straighten out all my problems. He just shook his head and said, "If you think you can fix what's wrong right now in your life, it's beyond being wrong. It's beyond fixable." And he started telling me the facts of my life as I was not aware of them.

"The police and the feds are looking for you because you hocked some of the stolen stuff beyond state lines. Your parents thought you were dead and don't give a shit anymore." (My father had been burned by me too many times.) Clark said, "There is no solution for you here in New York." He continued, "Why don't you go have a cup of coffee and a conversation with our friend Pamela?"

Pamela had just gotten back from Hazelden the year before. I figured he'd get off my back if I agreed to meet with her. Secretly, I thought this would give me the chance to work on him again to give me some dough.

I went to meet Pamela at a downtown restaurant and walked right into an intervention. I knew one when I saw one! And instead of being resistant as I had each time this was tried before, I collapsed, looked around the room, and said, "What time is my plane?"

Two or three people then drove me out to La Guardia Airport and put me on a plane with a one-way ticket to Center City, Minnesota. It had been arranged for me to have a bed at Hazelden. One of my ex-business partners was Steven Kalt. We had started our own consulting business. Steven kept my health insurance alive, against the other partners' wishes. They said, "No, let's not," but Steven said, "If he ever gets off the street. . . . Let's pay it for a year." It was literally day 360 or something. A freakish thing. In those days, insurance money was commonly available for rehab, unlike how it is today, and it paid for the lion's share. My friends all kicked in money for the rest, so off I went to Center City.

We had to get off the plane after my friend had left, because of some mechanical issue, so we had an hour to wait in the airport. They gave all the passengers some drink tickets, so I went right away to the bar and started ordering doubles. I got back on the plane nice and drunk. I had a twenty-dollar bill they had given me for cigarettes and a candy bar for the trip, and I used that to buy drinks on the plane.

I was sitting in an aisle seat, and there was a little old lady seated by the window. She kept looking at me and smiling. I was wearing smelly clothes and sunglasses. It takes weeks to wash the stink of the street out of someone who has been living the way I had been living. The lapels on my jacket had curled up from the tears I had cried. I sat there slamming down little bottles of vodka, and this lady kept looking at me and smiling. So I shot her my best scary New York City street guy look. Eventually, she leaned over, patted my leg, and said, "You're going to Hazelden, aren't you?" I looked at her and burst into tears.

I forget what it was: her husband had ten years and her brother had thirty, or her son had twenty and her nephew had fifteen, and her best friend was a volunteer there. She had like four connections to Hazelden within her family and friends. She looked at me and said, "Everything's going to be OK."

Unbeknownst to me, what she said was what enabled me to get in the car when the driver from Hazelden came to pick me up. I made it up to Center City and was on the medical unit for a couple extra days. I was touch-and-go from a medical standpoint. They finally brought me down to my unit. By this time I was so desperate, I could have sobered up in a liquor store. I was ready.

I just totally immersed myself in recovery. I thought it meant food and a clean place to sleep. I was sent to a placed called the Fellowship Club, and they told me that recovery was about what I was going to do to grow my spiritual life in a twelve-step program. I said, "You're crazy."

The second night there I went to my first recovery group meeting, in St. Paul. Uptown, 8 P.M., winter, very cold. A lady in a warm fur coat, very elegant, probably in her sixties, nice jewelry, good perfume. She looked like the mom you wished you had. And there she was, greeting people in the cold, on the sidewalk in front of the steps leading into the building. I sort of veered around her, but she leaned over and sort of lassoed me in with one arm, gave me a hug, and said, "Nice to have you here."

I hadn't heard "Nice to have you here" in ten years. No one said that to me. I went upstairs to the meeting and I was like a raindrop in a river. That was sixteen years ago.

They told me to get a sponsor; the next night I had a sponsor. He told me to go to meetings; I went to one every night. I immediately got myself involved and plugged in. I still have the same sponsor, and I still go to some of the same meetings. I used to think that I needed to put recovery into my life, but now I can't tell my life from my recovery.

My recovery life has changed significantly this year. I'm now on the road twenty-six weeks a year. I can't even sponsor newcomers—it wouldn't be fair to them or to me. I miss it, though: I used to sponsor a lot of guys. But newcomers need someone they see at meetings, someone they can sit down with at least once a week. Not someone like me who might be in the jungle somewhere, without a cell phone.

But one nice thing is I've gotten to go to meetings in China, Russia, the Philippines, and all over the world. I get to carry the recovery message in a different way now. I'm very transparent about my recovery. I'm respectful of the anonymity of the twelve-step program I'm involved in. I never talk about that. But I get up in front of people and say, loud and proud, "I'm sober today, and I'm a product of twelve-step recovery." So many people see drug addiction and alcoholism as the broken windowpane on the door when they get home at night, or the guy that mugged them on the street and stole their purse, which was me back then, or the crazy, homeless guy, which was me back then, too. But alcoholism is also me now. I now have a wife, a child, and cars in the garage. I'm a good citizen. I get to carry the message in lots of different ways, and I get to be an example of the Big Book in a much different way than I have previously. It's a really exciting time in my life and my recovery, because I'm no longer locked into St. Paul 365 days a year, the way I used to be.

In my recovery, I grew where I was planted. I put one foot in front of the other and developed the faith that my life would work out. The Big Book doesn't say that we are going to get rich; it says we will have freedom from financial insecurity. The way I learned the essence of my program from my sponsor was that I would feel

OK either with money or without money. People with sobriety either have successful careers or they don't. Life is just life. My sponsor says, "Life is fired at you from point-blank range." And it is.

I placed great importance on happiness. I thought it was my birthright to be happy all the time. Well, that's just not the way it is. I'm not happy all the time. But these days, I'm OK with not being happy, because I know that things are going to change. My wife and I have had times in our lives when we struggle to pay bills and times in our lives when we don't struggle to pay bills. I now know that happiness is not the be-all and end-all of life. It's more important to me to have my son know I love him, to have my wife know I love her, and to be able to experience their love for me than it is to bring home a big paycheck. If I keep myself right-sized, everything works in my life. Where I get bent out of shape is when my ego takes over and I stop communicating with my wife. I start to focus on what I don't have versus all the bless-ings I've received. I could not have had the career I have now, coming into the homes of millions of people in seventy countries on this box called a television, had it not been for my recovery. It couldn't have happened even after ten years of sobriety. I wouldn't have been ready.

In many ways I feel like a newcomer again, which is a great place to me. I often tell people I wish I could just recapture that sense of surrender I had when I walked in the doors of recovery meetings for the first time, when I would do anything to stay sober for ten minutes, let alone another day. I firmly believe there are people who deserve this program and its blessings more than I do, and there are people who need this program and its blessings more as well, who will never get it. Which means the most valuable piece of real estate for me isn't my home; it isn't some fancy hotel suite or the podium at some big event. It's that seat in that recovery meeting that I get to go to by choice. It's my choice to stay sober. I know I got sober 1-2-3, but I could slide out of it 3-2-1 if I'm not diligent. What keeps me sober is knowing that I need that seat as much after sixteen years as I did after sixteen days. I'm a product of my twelve-step recovery program, and because of that I know that I'm nobody special. Anyone—if they stay sober, go to meetings, show up for life, and tell the truth—can experience amazing things in life, as has happened to me. I can't explain it. There's no reason for it. It is simply God's grace.

I don't know why I've been given the blessing of my family. With my beautiful, amazing wife there's recovery in my home 24-7, 365 days a year. Our life is filled with recovery. The blessings I've received are available to everyone. I've seen it.

My wife and I joke that the one thing we'll never let a person we sponsor say to us is, "You don't understand." It's like, though we may look and smell different now on the outside, we're still recovering alcoholics on the inside, and we understand just fine. I was in Florida recently with a PR-marketing executive from a Fortune 500 company that sponsors my TV show, and she said, "Why did you move to Minnesota?" I told her I went there because I was a homeless junkie on the streets of New York who needed help, and my family and friends sent me to Hazelden. And she looked at me and said, "Yeah, right." She thought I was being funny and flippant and cute, and I said, "No, really, that's who I am." I told her that she must be one of those rare people that has no recovering person among her family or friends, and she said, "No, I don't." I said, "If you did, you'd know the stories."

It's all God's grace. I can't explain why I have the wife and son that I have or the career that I enjoy. I'm still filled with awe and wonder. The message that I like to tell is that when I got into my program, worked the steps, and my life changed, I began to have a relationship with God that was personal to me.

I've been in the program long enough now to have learned how to apply the principles to my work life, and that's when my career took off. They can be learned outside of recovery, but you learn all the better through suffering of some sort—stick-to-itiveness, fortitude, keeping the ego in check.

A woman from one of my groups in St. Paul once said to me, "If you don't start treating people in your work life like you treat people in recovery, you are going to be miserable the rest of your life." I've never forgotten that. I took a huge hiccup forward in my career when I started thinking about people I work with and people I work for as newcomers in recovery. I started listening better, looking them in the eye, and treating them like human beings, not trying to assert my dominance, like I was some ape in the forest. I thought my job was to put my foot on everybody's neck so I could float to the top of the shit pond.

It's like the minute I stopped looking at relationships with women as the vehicle to get me what I wanted, all of a sudden the most wonderful woman in the whole world walked into my life. That only happens when you export what you learn in recovery to other areas of your life.

As far as my career is concerned, I'm not sure I would have been able to navigate the road I'm on, just from a fear standpoint, to be able to give up the outcome of some of the stuff I've had come at me. No way. Not even at ten years sober would I have been able to say, "You know, I just did that screen test, or whatever, and whatever happens, happens." I couldn't do that. This coming Tuesday is the premiere of season number two of my show, and my network has invested a lot of money in it. Much more than ever before, and they're looking for good ratings. I'm thinking, "It's going to be what it's going to be." I couldn't have taken that vantage point at twelve years sober. Or fourteen or fifteen years. I also wouldn't have had the wisdom to know that when I return home from a long trip, and haven't seen my wife and son in two weeks, that my first night home is when my recovery begins with my family. That second night, I'm in a meeting. I also try to get to meetings on the road. I tell people I sponsor that you can always find a meeting. I was in the Amazon jungle, doing a shoot for my show, and I really needed a meeting. There were no meetings to be found. We were three days from anything. We were in a base camp in Ecuador on a beautiful lake, with jaguars in the forest and monkeys in the trees. We were out there with no electricity, with only a generator running our camp. All of a sudden, a guy walks into our camp—a Canadian bird-watcher and writer. So he joined us for dinner.

I said to the fellow, "Hey, glad you are here." I introduced myself. So we sit down and begin to eat. A server comes by, and I thought the bird-watcher was going to say, "I really need a drink—a glass of wine or something. It's been a long day." But he says to the server, "I'll have a club soda." Odd, the way he said it. I looked at him and said, "You don't drink?" To which he responded, "No," giving me an unusual look. I said, "You mean you don't drink professionally?"

And he said, "Yes." And I asked, "Are you a friend of Bill's?" I used to hate hearing that. But he said, "Yes, I am, and God, do I need a meeting!"

Can you imagine that? Two alcoholics in the jungle in Ecuador having a recovery meeting, sharing with each other their experience, strength, and hope. It was one of the best meetings I'd ever been to.

# 3

# Henry Pierce III

*Go upright among those who are on their knees*
*Among those with their backs turned and those toppled*
*   in the dust*
*You were saved not in order to live*
*You have little time you must give testimony*
—Zbigniew Herbert, "The Envoy of Mr. Cogito"

I first saw Henry Pierce III when he was introduced to give a eulogy for Michael Deaver at his funeral in Washington's prestigious National Cathedral. Michael was former president Ronald Reagan's chief of staff in the White House and a recovering alcoholic. His funeral was attended by more than two thousand people, including some of our nation's most powerful politicians.

Up to the podium, which hovered above the assembled crowd like a lectern in heaven, ambled this tall, heavyset, very dark-skinned man who looked ill at ease in the loose-fitting suit he was wearing. His husky voice contained the hint of a lisp, which seemed out of character, given his commanding presence—not unlike how Mike Tyson struck me when I first heard that baby voice of his.

Surveying the crowd before he spoke, Henry took his time before launching into his speech. It was as if he couldn't believe he was actually up there doing this. Once he got rolling, he was like a freight train, rambling along at greater and greater speeds.

The story he told not only captivated this seasoned audience but left us all shaking our heads in disbelief. It was one of those "can't get here from there" kind of stories, but rather than spoil it by revealing any of it here, I'll let Henry tell it himself. . . .

---

## HENRY PIERCE III

I'm trying to recall when I first started drinking. I think it was when my mother took me to this picnic in Washington, D.C., where I was born and raised. There was a case of Schlitz beer, if I remember correctly. Me and these kids started drinking, and I loved it: I thought the Schlitz was some magic potion or something. I took a few swigs, and it was nasty to the taste, but I got my first buzz. It was like, wow! We ended up stealing a couple of six-packs out of the case and scurried out into the woods with the beer. You see, I was this quiet little guy. I'm an introvert by nature, and a few Schlitz beers changed it all. I was able to be the life of the party. Everybody seemed to like me more. Whether it was true or not, I don't know, but it sure felt that way.

So that was kind of the beginning. I remember on the ride home I was in the back seat, and I leaned out the window and threw up all over the outside of the car. My mother had a fit. I was probably eight or nine years old when that happened—real young.

From that point on, I wanted to have that feeling again. I was always chasing that first drunk. Even at such a young age. My mother's boyfriend drank. He always kept something in the refrigerator, so every time I could, I would take a little something out of there. Drinking continued to make me feel free and uninhibited.

It took years for my using to progress. But then during the 1960s, when I was in my teens, the riots hit in D.C. after Martin

Luther King's assassination. All of a sudden the streets were flooded with soldiers and heroin. You could buy raw heroin, which was called a cap, or a doogie cap, back then. If you bought three they would cost a dollar each, which was known as buck action. One would cost two dollars, but if you bought three they were just a buck apiece. Buck action.

As an early teen, me and my boys would get our change together and we'd go get these caps and we'd snort them up, and man, that was another tier for me. We went from drinking Orange and Cherry Flip wine to snorting these little doogie caps. I snorted these for a while and started getting into a lot of trouble. My mother began to see a lot of changes in me, so she said, "I've got to do something with this boy," and decided to send me to military academy.

So off I went to St. Emma Military Academy in Rockcastle, Virginia. I was lower middle class, but a lot of the upper-class blacks went there. My mother mortgaged our house to send me to this private school.

I was there for a year. I got into the band and started getting kind of straightened out, but I also had a wild side. At the end of the year I begged my mother to let me come back to school in D.C. I guess she figured that I was doing all right, and considering the amount of money this was costing her, she agreed to allow me to come back home and go to school there.

My next experiment with drugs was back in D.C., when I went to a party with a couple of girls, and I followed the girl I liked into a backroom, where there was a big bowl of heroin in the middle of the bed, and they had these syringes sitting there, too. The girl said to me, "Henry, you've got to try this."

I was scared, but to keep this girl, I said, "Sure, sure." So I let some guy tie me off, and I put my little arm out there, and he hit me up. All of a sudden, this warm feeling goes up my arm and into my head and down all through my body. I remember thinking, "I don't know what this is, but I'm going to do this for the rest of my life." I loved it!

From then on I had a lot of mishaps, a few highs, and a lot of lows. I dropped out of school, I went into the military, then I dropped out of that. Though I ended up getting an undesirable discharge, because of Vietnam they upgraded it to a general discharge. Then began my life of crime. I was using so much dope that I had to begin selling to support my habit. So I started selling cocaine, marijuana, and heroin, and my fortunes started to turn.

By this time I had a decent job as a manager of an office supply store and had even met a girl, fallen in love, and gotten married. She knew nothing of my double life with drugs, but she wound up finding out soon enough once I started selling.

I ended up losing my wife. I wound up losing my job. I went down, down, down, very, very quickly. Finally, I ended up getting arrested for drugs, even though I considered myself a pretty successful and clever drug dealer. I was successful to my way of thinking, because when I was dealing, I could do whatever I wanted to do and made a lot of money while doing it. But soon enough, I got locked up for conspiracy to deal drugs. I was facing a double life sentence.

A young public defender straight out of law school in Boston was selected to be my lawyer. He was an idealist, out to save the world. Save the young black guys. It was a real lucky break for me because he worked his butt off on my case. Finally, we got a plea agreement for five to fifteen years, so off I went to the Lorton Reformatory in Lorton, Virginia. I did about four and a half years there, got out, committed more drug-related crimes, and went back to jail. I went back and forth numerous times, actually; I probably did six or seven more years total. The last time I got out, I was afraid that if I got busted again for a heavy-duty charge I would never see the light of day again. So out of fear of going to jail for life, I changed my ways—I started doing petty crimes like shoplifting and things like that, to support my habit. It's amazing to think that I considered this a radically new way of living. By this time, I spent a lot more money on using than I was able to make. Long story short, I wound up homeless on the streets of Washington, D.C.

Here I was, a guy who used to have good jobs. I was a manager of stores, even a bus charter company manager at one time. My mother was very intelligent. She worked in politics. I came from a very good home, was raised very well, yet I found myself homeless on the streets of D.C., living in abandoned buildings, and I just couldn't understand it.

Then, one cold morning, after many years of living this way, I woke up after sleeping on an old mattress with a dirty blanket on the floor of an abandoned building smelling of urine and feces with its windows busted out, and I thought, "What in the world happened to me?"

It was as though I woke up for that one brief moment and thought back on my life. The schools, the childhood, and again I thought, "What's wrong? How did I end up like this, on a dirty floor, smelling like feces, in an abandoned building?" And, as intelligent as I believed myself to be, I could not figure out how to get myself out of that situation. So I said a sincere prayer to the God I had always believed in but had never followed, asking him for help.

I had been hanging around in Chinatown, and there was a mission right down the street from the warehouse I was living in. A friend of mine who had been out on the streets with me was staying at that mission and had started to clean himself up. Next thing I knew, I am following him up the steps to something called the Metropolis Club—I had no idea what kind of club it was. They had a big pot of coffee in the back of that room and all these people sitting around talking. So I went in there and got me a cup of coffee and a stale doughnut. I got me a seat in the back and took a nap.

I started going to the Metropolis Club on a regular basis. Some guy started noticing me and one day walked over and said, "Welcome, man, you doing this, too?"

And I was like, "What am I doing? I came here to get me some coffee."

So that's what I continued to do. Later, I realized that they were having twelve-step recovery meetings there, so I'd go in, get my little coffee, and sit in the back of the room. I remember thinking, "Man, this is nice—and free." I'd return to my little abandoned building at night and have my wine and drugs between those meetings.

And then I decided to start listening at these meetings. I thought, "What are these people talking about anyway?" I started coming to in the last row of that meeting. People would say to me, "Keep coming back!"

So as time went on, I got more and more interested, although I still refused to surrender. There was this social worker that I used to go to that I would con out of bus tokens that I would sell to get money for wine. Wine was what I was drinking because I couldn't afford dope anymore. Wild Irish Rose wine, at that. Then one day I got real sick. I didn't know if I had AIDS or what was going on with me, so I went to the social worker and said, "Moe, I don't know. I think I messed up. I think I'm getting ready to die or something."

He told me, "If you decide to get some medical help, go down to this clinic called Health Care for the Homeless. If you go to the hospital, they're not going to give you proper care. They're gonna see the tracks on your arms because you're an addict, and they'll give you substandard care. But if you go over to this place I'm recommending, which is run by nuns, they'll give you some quality health care."

One morning I got up from sleeping in that abandoned building and I could barely walk and I thought of what that social worker told me. It took me an hour or so to walk the two blocks to the clinic. When I went inside I saw a doctor who took one look at me and knew I needed some help. So they took me to the back of the clinic and told me they were going to check me into their infirmary right now. That's when I knew I was going to die. What the doctor saw was that I was tired and it was time for me to come in out of the cold. So they placed me in the infirmary and took a lot of tests. They said that I was not seriously ill but that I was suffering from malnutrition and dehydration. I needed to drink a lot of water, get lots of rest, and eat regular nutritious meals.

I stayed in this homeless shelter infirmary for about a month, eating and getting my weight back. I had been skinny as a rail.

So after a while I was clearer in my mind and started thinking, "OK, where do I go from here?" I was attending these twelve-step meetings on a daily basis because it was a requirement. Then the doctor told me, "You know, it's not over for you yet. You need to go into treatment."

I said, "Treatment—what's that?" And he described a treatment program upstairs called New Way Recovery and told me that there were interviews coming up in a week. So the week passed and I went to the interview. The people were real nice. They asked if I was looking for help with my problem, and I surprised myself when I honestly said, "Yes, I am ready for my life to change, and I am tired of living the way I've been living."

So they gave me a date to return, and a meeting schedule, and they told me I had to go to twenty meetings, and when I did, I should come back and they'd let me into the program.

This was a stroke of luck. I went out and attended my meetings, and I came back and they told me I had been accepted into the program, that I didn't have to live like this anymore.

I was so high! I thought, "This is it!" I had finally found the track to get my life back together. That night I left the infirmary, went out and was walking to a meeting, when I came to this liquor store on the corner. Standing outside was this guy who I knew from the streets. I greeted him and started telling him how good my life was, that I was going into this program, how hopeful I was and so forth.

The fellow was holding a fifth of wine, and he looked at me and said, "You want some of this?" And before thinking at all, I took a drink, and I was immediately back to the races. It was as if none of the good stuff had happened.

A few hours later, the next thing I know I'm in Chinatown looking for some crack. Everybody I meet is saying, "Man, you look great! Where have you been? You got your weight on and those clean clothes. What's happening with you?"

I was like a star! Now I'm running around trying to hustle up some money. I met up with this girl that I knew, and me and this girl proceeded to get high. The next thing I know it was curfew time in the infirmary, so I went to try to sneak back in. I reach the front door, and the guard takes one look at me and starts shaking his head. He said, "Henry, I love you, man, but I can't let you in."

"What do you mean?" I asked. "Why can't I come in?"

He said, "Because you used."

"Look at me, I look just like I did this morning."

He said, "Come on, man, we both know you did."

I just could not understand how he knew I had gotten high. Anyway, the guard kicked me out, but he tells me, "Listen, you've been accepted into this program, so come back in two days and you can still get in."

So I go get that girl, and we are walking down from the shelter, and I run into this guy I know with his girl. They had been up in some alley hitting some crack. He tells me that he and his girl are getting a check in the morning: "A thousand dollars, and we need someone to cop for us. We got a room up the street at a rooming house, so you and your girl can come stay with us. We'll get this check, cash it, and you can go cop for us." I thought, "Man, that's a deal!" and I agreed to do it.

The next morning they got the check. We go down to the liquor store to cash it, and they give me the money. I go visit my guy about ten blocks away. My heart is pounding. "Oooh, we on now," I'm thinking. "This is a good day." So I took the stuff back to my friends, and we proceed to fire it up and get high all day long.

A strange thing happened then. Right away I noticed I wasn't getting high, I couldn't feel a thing. I was saying, "Hey, he beat us," and everyone else said, "Man, this is the best stuff I ever had."

They were twisted and I was mad. I didn't know what to do. I couldn't feel a thing. The owner of the rooming house we were in was a drunk. He yelled at me to come downstairs and talk to him. I thought, "Oh, Lord, he's gonna try and kick us out." But what he wanted was for me to go down to the liquor store and get him a case of beer. When I returned he asked me to sit and have a few drinks with him. He was talking about his life, and I was talking about mine. We became best friends in about an hour.

He told me that he had developed a drinking problem. "Some friends of mine were trying to talk me into going to those meetings."

I told him that I'd been going to meetings, so he asked me how come I stopped, and I said, "Because I have a problem, too."

I started telling him about the treatment program I was accepted into and that I was supposed to report tomorrow. So he says to me, "If you go to that program, I'll go to a meeting with my friend." I said, "You got a deal."

So about seven o'clock the next morning I picked my little butt up and started to walk on down there, and my new friend was still in the living room, and we waved good-bye to each other, and I've never seen him since that day.

But I went down to the program and there were about twenty people coming in just like me.

I walk in and there's this little white guy with a baseball cap on and a cup of coffee in his hand, and he says, "How are you doing? Welcome!" He handed me some coffee and a doughnut; we began talking.

I didn't know then it was Mike [Michael Deaver, former chief of staff in the Reagan White House]. I didn't know who he was for a long time. But I went into my interview with the founder of the program and they admitted me. It was called New Way Recovery (later changed to Clean & Sober Streets). Life started getting real good, real quick. Mike started bringing his friends in—people like former NFL star Hollywood Henderson—and I remember thinking, "Wow, these people are just like me. They have the same disease. And look at them, they're famous."

Mike got me this little landscaping job, just so I would have some money, after I'd been there a few months. One day the clinical director of Clean & Sober Streets came up to me and offered me the coveted volunteer position of detail manager of the facility. He said, "Every time I come by this bathroom you're in here cleaning it. Why?" And I said, "Because I like a clean bathroom." As time went on he came to me and said, "Come on back to the office. I'm going to talk to Julia and Andy, the program managers, and see if they can use your help in the office."

And that began my life in the administration of this drug treatment program. Me and Andy became real close. He was the development director, and he taught me a lot of things, about fundraising, politics, and the business of treatment. I was given my own little office. A while later Mike Deaver helped me through a temp agency to get a job at First American Bank, which eventually became First Union and, today, Wachovia Bank. I met a corporate vice president there who took me to lunch one day because he thought me to be a hard worker. I was working in the mailroom at the time. During lunch he says to me, "Tell me something about yourself." So I told him my story. He had no idea. The food just fell from his mouth.

When I saw the expression on his face, I thought, "Uh-oh, I just lost my job!" But the next day he summoned me up to his office on the top floor of our building, and he said, "Your story really moved me. To come from where you did to where you are today is remarkable. I would like to make you a job offer. I'd like you to come out to Virginia and head up our operations department (mail services). You'll probably want to move out there, so we'll give you a housing allowance to buy or rent a little townhouse."

In a way I was really excited, but I was also worried about leaving all my recovery brothers. While working at the bank downtown, I'd get off work, go to a meeting, then do my administrative work at night in the treatment center. All that would come to an end. My friends were telling me: "Don't be stupid. Think of the salary you'll be making." "You'd better take that job, man."

I continued to pray and meditate and finally made a decision. I went over to the vice president's office and told him, "I really appreciate the offer, but I think I'm going to go to work for Clean & Sober Streets full time." So I gave up this $50,000 a year job, which was a lot of money fifteen years ago, to come here and work for free.

Ever since that day I've been here, helping to develop this program. Soon I became program director; then when Julia and Marsh went into semiretirement, about seven years ago, I became executive director. Clean & Sober Streets began as a small social-model program with no clinical services at all. We used strictly twelve-step guidelines. We were a residential recovery program with no clinical treatment, just spiritual and loving recovery principles and structure. Yet our success rate was higher than average. When we decided to offer treatment, we needed licensing and certification, so my team and I started reading and doing research, going to school to get certified, and learning about grant writing so we could offer clinical services.

If you ask most people on the streets in D.C., they will tell you that we are running one of the most successful programs in Washington. We went from a small social model program, not making any money, to being among the top five treatment programs in the area. We compete for funds with the biggest programs in Washington, D.C. Not bad for being the little guys.

It was hard doing the work we had to do to make this a success, but it was harder containing my ego. Of course, at the time, I wanted to hear people say, "Henry did all of this," but that's not what happened at all. I finally figured out that it isn't about me. Henry is just an addict-alcoholic who found grace. The way to happiness for me is to be helping someone else.

# 4

# James L. Abernathy

*Thuse through the veryetye of changes the Lord was pleased to bring me to a seeming settled condicon, But a Lass our hyest rest here below is disrest and there is nothing under the sonn that can satisfie the soule of man.*

—ABRAHAM BROWNE, *JOURNAL*

James L. Abernathy is the founder and chief executive officer of the Abernathy MacGregor Group, a leading international financial communications firm with offices in New York and Los Angeles.

Describing Abernathy MacGregor's slant on PR, he says, "Like love, PR means a hundred different things to different people. We advise publicly traded corporations on dealing with issues in the investment community and other important constituencies."

Prior to establishing Abernathy MacGregor, he spent a decade at American Broadcasting Companies, the last three years as vice president of corporate affairs, with responsibility for all of ABC's corporate public relations, corporate advertising, external communications, and investor relations.

James, who began his career as an editor of several broadcasting trade publications, had previously spent two years as vice president for public and investor relations of Warner Communications Inc. and six years as a public relations and investor relations executive at CBS Inc. He is a past president of the Investor Relations Association and, while at ABC, was chosen by *Institutional Investor* as one of America's ten best investor relations executives.

He is a member of the board of the Caron Foundation, and it was his impetus that led to the establishment of Caron's New York Recovery Center. In addition, he is former chairman of Caron New York, director of the National Council on Alcoholism and Drug Dependence, a member of the board of overseers of the Brown University School of Medicine, a former director of Episcopal Charities, and a trustee emeritus of Hackley School.

He has been married twenty-seven years and has two stepdaughters and a daughter. Two of his children are in financial communications as well, one working in communications for a city councilman in Los Angeles and another at Comcast, while the third is a teacher. He is keen on getting old gracefully and staying active, which includes setting up programs for Cuba and Russia to make twelve-step work available to people who need it.

---

# JAMES L. ABERNATHY

I was born in Kansas City, Missouri, to an upper-middle-class alcoholic family. My mother and father were divorced four times, and I lived with my father during the winter in Missouri and later in Colorado, where he bought a big ranch. I went to the East Coast to live with my mother in the summers. I had multiple surrogate parents—stepmothers and stepfathers—and I was shipped around a lot. My time in Colorado was spent at a working ranch. My role models out there were the cowboys, the real sort of cowboys!

They wore Stetsons and jeans, and they spit on the floor. I thought they were really cool. My father's ranch was very far away from anywhere, so I was left to my own devices there. I drew and read a lot

My mother, on the other hand, married a New York lawyer shortly after divorcing my father and had two more children. This was the late 1940s. When I'd arrive at Idlewild (now JFK) Airport, she'd see this little cowboy get off the plane, and she'd drag me off to Brooks Brothers to clean me up and dress me like a Little Lord Fauntleroy. She'd also clean up my language and my accent until I was a quasi-acceptable little East Coast kid. Then at the end of the summer I'd get on a plane again and fly back to Colorado, where my father would see a Little Lord Fauntleroy at the airport. He'd shake his head and hurry me back to the ranch to turn me into a cowboy again.

The reason I tell this story is to point out that I had to adapt and adjust just like many kids of alcoholics have had to do. I learned to size up any situation in a nanosecond in terms of what I was supposed to deliver: whether I was supposed to be funny, whether I was supposed to be loving, whether I was going to get hit. Children of practicing alcoholics learn quickly.

In the interim if I ever was learning who I was, who Jim was, I lost it in the mix because I was so busy being a people pleaser. I learned how to deliver the goods on demand, and it became one of the dominant traits in my life.

After my mother got divorced again, my grandparents sent me off to a boarding school, Hackley, in Tarrytown, New York, where I went for four years. Meanwhile I had become quite an accomplished artist: a sort of political cartoonist and painter. I was art editor of our newspaper and even sold some of my paintings. I also thought of myself as an artist—and to an artiste almost anything is permissible! My core was as a creative person. That's what I was called at the time. People would say, "That's Jamie. He doesn't have to behave like the rest of us—he's creative." So that became part of my identity.

At Hackley I started drinking and I loved it. Like a cliché you hear from alcoholics, it made me feel whole. It made me feel attractive to women. I was funny and smart, and I could belong. You can't really describe that feeling to people who haven't had that experience. It's only other drunks, or highly neurotic people, who can identify with it. But it was powerful for me. Alcohol was my friend because it enabled me to function. But it was also my enemy because I smashed up cars, I got into fights, and I had terrible relationships with women and men.

In any event, I graduated from Hackley, sort of conning my way through. I was a smart kid. They liked my style. I was second in my class. So afterwards I went on to Brown University to pursue a fine arts degree. And by the way, it was at this time that my father killed himself because the huge ranch he owned in Colorado had gone bankrupt. He was a drunk and basically mismanaged it. By this time, my mother was broke. So, though I came from a very affluent family, I became virtually broke myself. It was my grandfathers who, when I got into Brown, came forward and paid the freight. I was going to be an artist. I figured in the field of commercial art or cartooning. At Brown was the first time I had complete freedom and girls around. Previously I had attended a boys' boarding school. I also had complete access to booze. So I went nuts!

I loved it there. I loved the freedom, the booze, and the girls, and I spent the next five or six years getting thrown out and readmitted into Brown. Thrown out because I didn't show up. I didn't do the work; I just tried to bullshit my way through. When it got competitive, I completely lost it. I'd drink and go to parties. I was thrown out of Brown four times.

In the interim I had some jobs and went to Harvard and Boston University summer schools, where I got A's. I also joined the Marines as an officer candidate and went to summer training. I thought it was a very cool idea. I would become a second lieutenant in the Marines. Korea was over and Vietnam was yet to come. And like most jerk-off eighteen-year-olds who need to prove themselves, I wanted this arena to do it in.

So I did the Marine thing because I wanted to see if I could do it. I did well, but since I didn't graduate college, I didn't get a commission, so I went into the Reserves for six years. Never really did active duty. Instead, I was a weekend warrior.

Then I came to New York looking for a job. I thought I could be an advertising guy or a writer for *Time* magazine or something. I spent a lot of time waiting in reception areas at ad agencies but never got offered a job. Seldom got an interview because there wasn't a huge demand for people who had been thrown out of Brown several times—I didn't have a great track record. So I was kind of desperate when finally I got a job with a trade magazine called *Television Age*. In the interim I had married a woman I had gone to Brown with, who was also a drunk. We drank together. She became one of the first women stockbrokers. We stayed together for four or five years; then I ran off with my secretary.

I did these things because I never really figured out who I was. I never really had a role model for what an adult male should be like. I was playing it by ear. One part of me identified with the Boy Scout I once was. I liked being helpful, friendly, courteous, kind, obedient, et cetera—all that good stuff. The other part of me identified with the darker side of life—I had once read *Othello* in school, and I remember how cool I thought Iago was. I was split between being the evil manipulator and being a goody-two-shoes Boy Scout. I flipped back and forth, like from Colorado and New York. I flipped back and forth, confusing others and myself.

Also, whatever I was wasn't good enough. Therefore I always had to inflate one thing or another. So I ran off with my secretary instead of our having a mild and passing flirtation.

I had moved by this time from the magazine to CBS, where I worked for six years. I had seen contemporaries, people close to me, who were amusing or cute alcoholics at eighteen or twenty become loony or go down into full-blown dementia.

I never really got into drugs, but I was getting prescribed drugs for my depression, for my "Gee whiz, I don't know who I am" condition, and I would use them in conjunction with booze.

They say two plus two equals four, but with these drugs it was two plus two equaled one hundred. I was bouncing around acting crazy. A real lunatic! At that time I was at ABC. I was introducing the president of ABC to a group of security analysts. I had taken my whole combination of booze and antidepressants, and I stood up and said to Tony Themopolis, head of ABC, "Tony, you are cute. You are so cute." And I went on and on. Remember, this is a group of security analysts. Everyone thought I was either a bad stand-up comedian or demented.

Anyway, I had several bad experiences like this. Mostly personal, not so much in the professional arena. Grandiosity got to me in the midst of this, too, as I kept slipping between being "poor little Jim" and this showbiz biggie. In that little universe at ABC—in advertising, corporate affairs, and financial—I was a very big deal; I, Jim Abernathy of ABC, was one of the cooler people you could meet at a cocktail party.

Howard Cosell was my good friend; because I didn't know or care anything about sports, he would seek me out. We would have breakfast regularly and wouldn't ever talk about sports, which made him very happy. I was sort of a shadow for the great and near-great, and I really got off on that stuff.

I was good at my job, very good. I got promoted and I manipulated, and ABC was a good place to manipulate.

Again, I only worked for the chairman, the president, and the CFO.

In 1979, when I had been at ABC four years, the burden of being me, keeping my act together and drinking whenever I could, was getting to be too great—to tap dance, remember what I had said, and keep my stories straight. And part of my job was entertaining people, taking them to the Four Seasons, Twenty-One, et cetera. Pouring wine and booze down their throats and mine. I had broken up with my girlfriend—or rather, she had broken up with me. I tried to commit suicide: I took a lot of pills, drank some booze, and then called somebody on the phone. An inauthentic attempt, like everything else in my life. I don't think I ever did anything authentic.

So my doctor sent me to the Lenox Hill Hospital. I was looking up at the ceiling of the emergency room while my M.D. told me, "You know, Jim, you're not crazy—you're an alcoholic."

I would much rather have been crazy. "Crazy" was interesting. "Crazy" was creative. "Crazy" was cool. "Alcoholic" was none of these.

This was 1979, before people were lined up to go into rehab. So I ended up going to Chit Chat Farms for twenty-eight days. The fellow who founded Chit Chat, Dick Caron, used to meet with people in his kitchen, sort of like Bill W. from the Big Book; he would have coffee and conversation with them. He was a very powerful role model for many. Initially, the place was called Chit Chat Farms, but when I got on the board a number of years later, I pointed out that it was very difficult to try and raise money in New York for something called Chit Chat. So in the mid-'80s the name was subsequently changed simply to Caron, after Dick Caron.

I didn't tell ABC that I was a drunk. Instead, I told them that I hadn't had a vacation in a couple of years, which was true. In that culture I either didn't stand out as a drunk or I covered it well. Or both. There was no perception professionally that I was a drunk.

So I went to Chit Chat Farms for twenty-eight days. Here I was a network television biggie in the hills of Pennsylvania, with all these hicks with their funny Bucks County accents. People who were making $19,000 a year. I was pretty contemptuous of them and of what was going on. How uncool this all was, but I did listen. When I left after twenty-eight days, I was voted "the most unlikely to stay sober," due to my grandiosity and arrogance.

I came back to New York and paid attention to some of the things I learned at Chit Chat Farms: Watch out for people, places, and things. Stay away from my girlfriend because she could push my buttons. Stay away from my mother. Stay away from x, y, and z. But first and foremost, shut up and go to recovery program meetings—and I did that. I got assigned a sponsor. He told me, "If you want to get sober, you'll do what I tell you, and if you don't, that's your business, but don't come to these meetings. We know what will get you sober. Going to meetings will get you sober."

So I spent a lot of time doing twelve-step work. As a new-comer, I cleaned up cigarette butts—that's when you could smoke at meetings. I had lost about forty pounds when I was at Chit Chat Farms, so I thought, "Not only will I kick booze, I'll kick weight, too." I got down to about 170 pounds (I'm five-foot-ten). I ditched my girlfriend, avoided my mother, and I felt good! I looked good, too. Got my job back. Felt that everything was cool, that I was handling everything pretty well, although I still had not gotten sober at that point. I was dry but not sober.

I made a couple of friends in the meetings in those early days, and I showed up with one of these new friends at the Macy's Thanksgiving Day Parade. How corny! He had a couple of kids, so we stood there on some corner watching the balloons go by. For some reason, it was at that moment that I truly started to surrender to my disease and take the first real step of becoming sober. All of my repressed emotions became unstuck, and I was standing there watching a corny parade while tears were flowing down my cheeks. This guy, who was maybe six months ahead of me in recovery, said to me, "Jim, you don't ever have to feel this bad again. I've got a secret for you." He put his arm around me and said, "Don't drink. And go to meetings." All of a sudden, for the very first time, this made perfect sense.

You just never know what combination of events is going to finally get your attention. Going to rehab got my attention on one level, but it hadn't hit me viscerally. So I did what he told me to do and went to a lot more meetings and did a lot more service. I got a couple of sponsors—a board of directors, in effect. All of a sudden my life improved miraculously. I kept my job and was doing well in that. I looked and felt great. I was dating a tremendous number of women. Remember, this was the mid-eighties when women were discovering whatever they were discovering. I was a willing tool for their discovery process.

Then I did a couple of things that went against what I had been told. At about six months sober I met this incredible woman at a dinner party, and despite the fact that you're not supposed to make changes or do anything different for a year or two, I fell immediately in love with her. She left her husband and two children and ran off with me. We got married and had our own child, who's now twenty-five. It hasn't been easy, but it's been a spectacular marriage. A year or so later, all of the manipulation and bad blood I had created at ABC in my climb to the top came to a boil and hit me good, and I was fired.

So there I was, a new child, my wife, a big mortgage, and no income. My wife and my program put their arms around me and said, "Jim, we know you, we love you, and don't worry, it's going to get better . . . one day at a time."

By then I had about a half-dozen really close friends from my program, most of whom are still alive and I see regularly. They held my hand and made me feel that it was possible for me to get out of this mess. This was the first time sober that I had contemplated suicide because I felt my reputation was never going to recover. No one would ever hire me again. I remember applying for little crapola jobs, including one out in Minneapolis paying $60,000, when I had been making $400,000 at ABC in those days. I was trying to convince myself that I could live in Minneapolis on $60,000 a year.

Fortunately, I didn't get the job. Instead, what I started doing, thanks to a few friends, was consulting. Abernathy Consultants is what I called it. A couple of friends paid me for PR and financial public relations advice. That was 1984, twenty-four years ago. Since then my business has gone very well. I have sixty people working here and a dozen in California; I also have offices in Europe. I sold this firm six years ago to a French holding company called Hermes. They paid us a lot of money and kept me as chairman, so I still run the business. We do a good job and bring in a lot of money for them. We do a lot of crisis management for companies; I've got a great group of senior executives here—about ten of them, who are really smart and know what they are doing.

My whole professional life has been as a behind-the-scenes guy in the PR-communications business for the great and the near-great. I worked as head publicist for Steve Ross for a couple of years and then went to ABC as a corporate PR stiff for ten years, and I worked at CBS also behind the scenes for six years and at Warner for two. Now I run a PR firm for corporate stiffs; we represent Viacom and a lot of entertainment and communications people on the corporate side. We help them work with Wall Street.

It's not always a random walk through silliness. We often have a plan. I have a considerable number of other clients, including airlines and financial service companies. For me, what I still engage in is the entertainment side. As you know, once you played around on that turf, it's hard to disengage.

So what has changed is that I learned how to tell the truth. I remember one incident when my colleagues Ted Ashley and Steve Ross and I went to an analyst meeting of Capital Research, money managers in California. I had talked to the money managers there and said, "What do you want to hear?" (This was in 1972.) They replied, "We think Steve is a genius, but we don't buy this whole cable television story. We think Steve is spending entirely too much money, squandering resources on the entertainment business."

So I said to Steve, in briefing him and Ted, "When you are in our meeting, don't spend too much time on cable. Don't turn that into the focus of your whole presentation. They want to hear about your total vision for the company."

Promptly Steve, as soon as he opened his mouth, did a big thing on cable. In the limo on the way back, Steve said, "Well, how did I do, Jim?" And I said, "Well, Steve, I thought it was good, it was interesting. You spent a lot of time on cable, but you're a brilliant guy. . . . Blah, blah, blah."

Afterwards we were at the Beverly Hills Hotel and Ted said, "Jim, I want to have a drink with you. [This was before I was sober.] I was at both meetings, when you briefed Steve and afterwards, and you're never going to be any good to yourself or anyone else unless you tell him the truth, as painful as it is."

I said, "Thank you, sir, but he's Steve Ross and just a little nothing." And Ted said, "No, I'm sure you have to learn this."

Ten years later I reminded Ted of that story. I saw him at a dinner and he had no memory of it. I told him that it was one of the high points of my life. In any event, what has happened is that I have now made a career of telling the truth. Of not being intimidated by authority. Of course we all want to be liked, and I have problems from time to time with my clients, but I have the sufficient sense of myself to be able to say to the CEO, "You know, Charlie, I don't think this is going to work for you. Here are some alternatives, but what you are contemplating doing is really destructive: don't do it!"

Sometimes they say, "OK." Other times they say they are going to do it anyway. And sometimes they say, "Get the hell out of my office!" But I can go home at night not feeling that I sold my soul for a pound of something or other. And in my business, we don't do product PR, and nothing is "the greatest." We get paid to tell corporate CEOs what the reality is. Mostly that is because their in-house people are too busy kissing their ass, and the top people tend not to believe them.

So, for a guy who was always a people pleaser, I've developed some character. I'm certainly not perfect—two steps forward and one back—however, I'm a much more comfortable person now than I was.

I attribute the improvement to several factors. Essentially to my twelve-step program. Part of it has been understood as aging. What was insanity, or stupid, or smart ass when I was twenty-five is now profound at sixty-seven. Other people take me seriously because of my gray hair—or no hair—and they figure I know what I'm doing. But mostly it's because I'm not afraid to displease somebody. I could be wrong, but I get paid for telling my clients what I think is the best approach. And that's valuable to a client because we get into some very "front-page" stories in the business press—transactions, fights, et cetera—and we have to be tacticians and strategists for them and get them through stuff on a day-to-day basis. Clients rely on our judgment and our ability to tell them the truth, whether it is awkward or painful or something entirely different for them.

My daughter, who is twenty-six, went to Brown. Five years and she fell down a flight of stairs with her head filled with cocaine and booze. She was in the hospital for a while. I sent her to rehab at Father Martin's, not Caron because I'm so involved in Caron. And now she's four-and-a-half years sober, and if you want gratitude, it's seeing this child grow and become once again the wonderful person she was when she was twelve. A genuine, smart, decent kid after a long period of deterioration. It's been a great gift for me to see that.

I'm very active for Caron. Brown University actually gave me an honorary degree about six years ago, and I sit on the board of their medical school. Doctors at Brown have been working on a cure for alcoholism. They are trying to find a goddamn pill or an isolated gene they can cap and then we won't be alcoholics anymore.

For me, the twelve-step program works and I can't countenance anyone throwing a bunch of pills at the disease. In any event, that's one area in which the board I sit on is involved.

I took Caron to Russia in 1990, and we opened the first outpatient rehab in Moscow. I went to Cuba and brought rehab information down there. We brought a Cuban back and had her trained at Caron. I need to be reminded all the time that I'm an alcoholic. It's not just going to meetings. It's also my Caron work. I have an excellent marriage, wonderful family, and great business. I need reinforcement that I'm a drunk and I could lose all of this. I feel good about myself most of the time. I feel as though I'm doing the right thing. I haven't had a relapse; I feel so much gratitude. Of all that has happened in my life, the factor that was the principal change in course has been my twelve-step program. I'm not talking about being dry; I'm talking about being sober. Working the twelve-step program.

I'm sixty-seven. Five years ago I had a heart operation and almost died. I had to come to peace with myself. I came to accept that if I died I would have left my campsite a lot cleaner than how I had found it—the Boy Scout in me has prevailed. I spoke at Caron recently and told them that I have three parts to my sobriety. One is stopping drinking, which I did at Caron. The second stage was figuring out what getting sober meant, understanding how much work I had to do. And the first two were leading to the hardest, which was leading a sober life day to day. Not being an asshole, while trying to do what I'm supposed to do each day. Plus I do a lot of work with other alcoholics. It's good for them, and it's great for me.

# 5

# David Dashev

*As soon as she the fiend did name,*
*He flew away in a blazing flame.*

      —"Riddles Wisely Expounded," in *Popular Ballads*

When you'd put David Dashev and me in the same room, you could often see the sparks fly. It would be like two fighting cocks circling and appraising each other. It took only a few seconds before one of us was shaking down the other to determine the quantity and type of drug he was in possession of. "I *know* you're holding, man. Give it up."

We were usually forthright with each other. If I was "in pocket" I would usually share my good fortune with David, and he would cough up something for me as well. There were times, however, when no amount of coaxing would get either of us to reveal, let alone share, our stash. If we were running low on supply, or were "Jonesing," we'd say and do anything to keep what we had for ourselves.

But more often than not, supply was not the problem. I remember a particularly bountiful night at David's small rustic home in the semi-posh Nichols Canyon section of the Hollywood Hills. I had come to visit David, as I often did, to sit, have a few laughs, maybe listen to some music, but most of all, to get lit up with him. After a few joints and some good quality coke, we started fantasizing, as we often did, about story ideas we thought would make a good movie. This is how David and I worked. Get high . . . talk story. Several hours and many grams of cocaine later on this particular night, a little confection of a storyline that would eventually become the motion picture *The Fish That Saved Pittsburgh* was born.

David is one of the brightest and most talented guys I've ever known or worked with. I'm so glad he found his way into recovery and was willing to share his remarkable story, including the birth of *The Fish That Saved Pittsburgh*, with us.

---

# DAVID DASHEV

I had what you would call an uneventful childhood. I was born in the blue-collar town of Jersey City, New Jersey. Neither of my parents had any substance abuse issues. In fact, the only alcohol I ever saw was at Passover seders. I'm what you call a culinary Jew. Our family heritage goes as far back as the dining room table. So, I saw wine, but that was it.

I'm an only child, and my parents doted on me. From my earliest recollection I knew what I wanted to get and I knew how to achieve it. And it was accomplished without any regard for the truth. I knew what my parents wanted to hear. I knew what they expected and my job was to deliver that.

I didn't do any drugs in high school, but when I was seventeen I made the decision to go as far west as I could for college, since I had never been west of Newark. So, in 1963, I applied and got accepted to Occidental College, a small liberal arts school in California. It was a great time to be there. My social consciousness, which at this time had just begun to develop, really took off in L.A. In the air was a lot of change, political activism, and marijuana, a potent mix. I started experimenting with marijuana at this time and started hanging out on the Sunset Strip, where it was all happening. During my senior year at Occidental, not only was I the student body president, but I became a contributing editor at the *L.A. Free Press*, which at the time was the bible of the counterculture. I was also a tutor for kids in Watts. I would go there three nights a week, come back, go to school, and on the weekends hang out with my friends, smoke some dope, and bitch about politics. That's what my life was until I graduated in 1967, just in time for the Tet Offensive in Vietnam.

Anyway, I found out I was about to be drafted, so I applied to graduate school at Harvard University and I got in. I was getting a Ph.D. in black American literature, even though I was white and Jewish. I like to think of myself as the white Barack Obama. He went to Occidental College and then to Harvard, just like me. Thank God he didn't pattern the rest of his life after mine!

I moved to Cambridge to attend Harvard. Another hot bed of marijuana. I got my master's and chose to go back and teach in Watts in order to avoid getting sent to Vietnam.

Teaching in Watts solidified the feeling that I was living in the margins. The far end of the margins. I was regularly getting stoned, smoking marijuana after school. I was now married to my high school sweetheart. She was teaching in an elementary school in Watts. I was teaching at Jordan High School and writing music reviews for local papers.

Soon, I got a job writing for a friend of mine who was the music editor at the *L.A. Times*. It was great. I got to immerse myself in the world of rock 'n' roll and eventually became the publication's number two music critic.

I also became a big cocaine addict. Began using large quantities of the stuff and pretty much stayed stoned 'round the clock. I still thought I was making a political statement by getting high. My powers of denial were gigantic, inverse proportionately to my powers of insight. I realize now as I look back on it that I needed to feel like I was doing something positive.

Not long after this, my father had a heart attack, and I moved back to New Jersey to be with him. Shortly after I moved back I was walking down a street in Jersey City when I heard an a cappella record being played in a small record store. I had never heard anything like that, so I walked in and asked the clerk about it, and he told me it was a tape of a live concert. I learned that the group performing was called the Persuasions and they were from the Bedford-Stuyvesant section of Brooklyn. I somehow got a meeting with them and convinced them to record something, which I then took to L.A. to try and sell to Frank Zappa, whom I had met and had reviewed in the *L.A. Times*. Frank loved them, so we made a deal and I brought the Persuasions to L.A. for a live showcase performance.

After the show I got very loaded, and the group said to me, "You're supposed to be the straight businessman and we are supposed to be the screwed-up artists." That was the beginning of the next five years of my life. I stayed on the road with the group. I loved the whole music scene. I was doing all kinds of drugs (except for psychedelics, which scared me too much). Over the course of the next five years I produced twelve albums with the Persuasions, taking them from record label to record label because nothing they recorded was selling.

My experience with the Persuasions did get me a good job at A&M Records as a record promoter. Now, my life was in clubs; every night, promoting records and looking for new talent. By this time my cocaine use was totally out of control. I would go into restaurants, order food, lay out lines of coke on the table, and only eat desert. I thought that's what everybody did. I didn't know anyone who didn't get high. There was no intervention from friends because everyone I knew got high like me.

Next, I started occasionally using heroin, and I eventually stopped doing cocaine, going to heroin full time. During that period I quit the record business because my good friend Gary Stromberg had produced a movie called *Car Wash*, and I saw what he had done and thought, "This is really cool," and what I really wanted to do was be a writer. So I wrote a screenplay about my life with a college friend named Stuart Birnbaum. He showed me how to write; I showed him how to use heroin.

We wrote the screenplay and thought it was great, but the studio thought it was too edgy. After three rewrites the project stalled. The studio offered us a chance to write another film, though, *Smokey and the Bandit II*, which has the distinction of not having Burt Reynolds in it! We wrote that for a shitload of money, and I found out a lot about how the movie business works.

They were shooting *Smokey and the Bandit III* in Florida, so they flew us there, put us up on a houseboat, and wanted us to do a rewrite. They asked us, "What do you need?" All we really needed was an eight-ball of cocaine every day and some heroin to bring us down from the coke. That's how the rewrite got done. They paid us $25,000 for four days of work, which almost covered my FedEx bill for sending in drugs from L.A. The studio head of security sold me a 38-special, because "everyone in Florida needs one."

So there we were, totally jacked-up, sitting on a houseboat with a gun. I remember one time, it was around three o'clock in the morning, and I decided to go fishing. We didn't have any poles so we used the 38. I shot two bass. It wasn't a "catch-and-release" program. I was completely out of control. A real mess.

When I came back from Florida my life started going downhill really quickly. I had gotten my fifteen minutes of fame, so I was given lots of work. But that's not what I was looking for. I was the kind of writer who loved "having written" but didn't enjoy the actual writing. It didn't help that Stuart and I were into heroin full time now, no cocaine. The work started slowing down. I remember one day our agent called to tell us about this movie they needed a writer for called *Police Academy*. They were thinking about hiring us and wanted us to come to a meeting at the studio. I was at a 7-Eleven at a pay phone, waiting for the dope man to deliver my daily supply, so I had to evaluate my priorities. I chose to wait for my dealer and blew off the meeting. I think they made seven *Police Academy* movies, which we could have been part of, but I knew what I needed at the time. I was circling the drain.

Then, my old pal Gary Stromberg and I were sitting around one day and came up with an idea for a movie about basketball. We both loved the game, and we both loved music. He had a major success with *Car Wash*, and the idea we came up with became the movie *The Fish That Saved Pittsburgh*. It was the easiest sale we ever made, and this little movie occupied the next chunk of my life. Gary and I took turns outdoing each other in degradation and drug use. The production office for the movie was like a carnival of insanity. We were always high. We interviewed actors and directors, the things you do when you produce a movie, but we were fueled by insane amounts of drugs.

By this time, my wife and I had split up. She moved back to New York while I was becoming a film producer. A great job for a junkie. Gary and I went to Pittsburgh to shoot the movie, which had all of the great professional basketball players of the time in it. We had a first-time film director, who needed a steady hand for guidance and Gary and I were it, even though we made no sense at all. The movie did get made, in spite of us. I remember Gary was asked to leave the film set for a while because of his out-of-control drug use, which was funny because the studio thought he was the problem. They left me, the one with no film experience, to run the show. I didn't worry about the consequences or my inability to make a movie. All I thought was, "This is great. I can do his dope *and* mine."

Afterwards, I returned to L.A. and wrote a couple more film scripts. Horrible stuff, though I was still hirable, but not for long. *The Fish* came out in 1981, and the next five years are kind of a blur. In 1986 my wife is gone, I'm living in a small house in the Nichols Canyon section of L.A., and my life is about getting up in the afternoon and going out to cop drugs. I don't have any money, though every once in a while I get mailbox money, also known as a royalty check, because the movies I worked on are still playing somewhere. I also have no friends. I'm reduced to dealing drugs to white boys that don't have a connection. I'm buying dope in downtown L.A., stepping on it, and reselling it to guys in Hollywood. I'm also on three methadone detox programs at the same time. I'm selling my methadone and buying dope with the money I get.

Around this time a friend of mine tells me that I look like "one of the walking dead," and he takes me with him to Australia, where he was building a house. That's when some serious withdrawals started to kick in. I was throwing up along the journey, and when we got to Australia, I threw up for about three weeks. It was the worst detox you could imagine, but after three weeks, I was clean. It was the longest period I had gone without heroin in years.

My friend put me to work on his marijuana plantation, which was great, because I wasn't smoking at the time. I worked there for about four months and stayed in Australia for a year. I came back to L.A. to get my visa renewed. Was there for two nights, met a girl, and brought her back to Australia with me. A year later we returned to L.A. I was clean. I did not get high that whole year in Australia.

But I only stayed clean for four days in L.A. There was a writers' strike going on. I was out of work, but I had just gotten another royalty check, and I proceeded to go off to the races one more time.

My friend Stuart, I discovered, was now in recovery, and he took me to my first twelve-step meeting. It was sort of a rogue meeting, with a lot of people I knew from the entertainment business there—including Gary. I remember being very impressed with that meeting, but not impressed enough to want to stop using. In fact, the meeting was so intense I had to get high afterwards. But at that meeting, I did see some things I didn't know existed. I saw that some people I really respected had found a way to live without drugs. I wasn't ready to live like that yet, but it made an enormous impression on me. The thing I most remember is that all of a sudden Gary and Stuart, my two best friends, who had used as much as I did, had this wisdom, making sense of their lives' experiences, and they had a perspective and overview that just blew me away. I'm thinking, "I've been getting messed up and they've been getting smart. Where did these guys learn this stuff?" I didn't know it at the time, but it was coming right from their twelve-step program, but they seemed to be so at ease and at peace. No goody-two-shoes stuff. It was just that these guys got smart.

Soon after this meeting, I got a call from the New York state police telling me that they had found my ex-wife's decomposing body on the side of the road near Syracuse, New York. This was the woman I had grown up with. The woman who had attended my bar mitzvah. I was stunned.

One of the few pieces left on her body was a locket with my name on it, so the police were able to contact me. I learned that since we had broken up, she had met a guy—a bad guy, a felon. They were making a dope deal and then they were going to the Bahamas. The guy actually had the nerve to call me, in an attempt to create an alibi. I told the police about this, and they eventually caught him in a sting operation. They jailed him, and two weeks later I got a call telling me I would have to appear at the trial. It would happen nine months down the road. This was probably the second big incentive to get clean. My beloved wife was dead. She had been strangled and covered with duct tape; she had then aspirated on her own vomit. I saw the coroner's photos and it was just awful. If that wasn't a wake-up call, I don't know what was.

I was still getting high, but I wasn't laughing anymore. I was just self-medicating at this point. After the trial, which happened sooner than I'd expected, I flew back to L.A. and made a determined effort to get clean.

By this time I was three months behind on my rent; I was eventually to move into the back seat of my 1986 Audi. I went and scored seven days' worth of heroin. I put it in little bottles marked Monday, Tuesday, Wednesday, et cetera, and I decided to skip town and drive to Florida where my father was living. He never knew I did drugs. He just thought I had the flu for twenty years.

Of course, I shot up all seven bottles of heroin the first night. Along the way to Tallahassee, I went back and forth into Mexico six times, from Tucson, Nogales, El Paso, et cetera. I visited every ER I could find in Mexico, claiming nasty, soft-tissue back pain that wouldn't show up on an MRI. Each one of these places gave me a couple of Percosets, a couple of Vicodin, or other painkillers. Anyway, I arrived in Florida, thirty days later, totally clean. It was the worst detox I'd ever been through. It almost killed me. I was vomiting blood.

I arrived at my dad's house and stayed there for about a week, and then I decided to get high again. I couldn't stand the pain, but I didn't know where to score. I drove to Delray Beach, which is a hotbed of recovery, and found a recovery meeting. I had it planned. I would go in there, and somebody would tell me where to score. So I walk in, and it's a meeting filled with these tough bikers! So I wander over to the back of the room, "the isle of denial," and turn to this guy next to me, and I say, "How you doin'?" And he says, "Why are you here?" I answer, "Because I got a drug problem." He says, "No, man. You're here because you have a drug answer." And it was one of those lightbulb moments that I couldn't spin any other way except to say, "Yeah, I have a drug problem." He says again, "You got a drug answer, for every problem, and on top of that, you're full of shit." So I ask him, "What can I do about it?" And he says, "Come back tomorrow."

That was it. I was hooked. He told me to do a 90 and 90; I did a 240 and 240. I would go to the 7 A.M. meeting, the noon meeting, and then an evening meeting. My dad never knew what was going on. I told him I was looking for work. I'd put a suit on and go to a meeting, and then I'd change clothes and lay out at the beach. I would hang out with people from the meetings. These guys were as smart as Gary and Stuart had been. They knew me. They really knew me. In fact, I bought a notebook and I sat in the back of the meetings and I took notes. I wrote down every phrase, every bumper sticker slogan, all of it, because I didn't want to miss any of it. My first year I averaged three meetings a day. It was all about the program and learning how to live clean.

Eventually, I got a job teaching school, and that led me to getting offered a position teaching in a hospital drug unit. Then to me being made program director of that unit and, eventually, being the administrator of the psychiatric hospital. I remember when I had my interview—this company is the largest hospital provider in the United States—and the person interviewing me said, "I see you've done a lot of things personally and professionally. What are you most proud of?" I looked right at him and said, "When I stopped using heroin." There was this sudden silence. I realized at that moment that I needed to be completely open about my life. Being secretive wouldn't work for me. I was fueling my first year of recovery on self-loathing, but now I wanted the world to know I was an addict in recovery.

A recovering drug addict became my entire identity for the next fifteen years I ran that hospital. I was very open about my addiction. I loved my new life. I left the hospital four years ago, and with my old writing partner Stuart, we opened a company called Meditox, which does outpatient opiate detoxes. We've become a national company with offices all over the country. This business has become tremendously successful. A short time ago the chairman of the department of psychiatry from my former hospital and I started a consulting company where we treat high-profile addicts and alcoholics: executives, professional athletes, celebrities, most of whom have failed in previous attempts at recovery. We do individual therapy with them for five hours a day. One-on-one.

Nothing that I do today is as hard as living the lie I used to live as an active drug addict. Reinventing myself on a daily basis, depending on who I was talking to. I'm not afraid of being honest today. The hardest thing I ever did was stop shooting dope, and because of what I went through, nothing scares me anymore. There's almost nothing I can't handle, and if I can't handle it, I'm not afraid of saying I can't handle it.

# 6

# Maggie Sherman*

*Lives of great men all remind us
We can make our lives sublime;
And, departing, leave behind us
Footprints on the sands of time.*
—Henry W. Longfellow, "A Psalm of Life: What the
Heart of the Young Man Said to the Psalmist"

My navigational system, Mapquest, is accurate without being illuminating, so it was an odd phenomenon to "drive on water" across the Annapolis Bay twin bridges to meet Maggie. With a shore-to-shore length of 4.3 miles, the bridges are among the world's longest, most scenic, and, for many, scariest over-water structures.

Maggie had told me when I drove down from Connecticut and stayed in Baltimore that I'd have to farther trek to eastern Maryland. But as I have something of a view of the world that Saul Steinberg depicted in his drawings—except for me it is the corridor of I-95 that defines the greater part of my travel—eastern Maryland didn't register more than . . . isn't that Rehoboth Beach? She graciously offered to meet me in D.C. or Baltimore, but I

*Name has been changed.

had a feeling that when interviewing a powerhouse of industry, it would be advantageous to hear her story when she was at leisure, at home.

Her home is at a magnificent point near Annapolis, surrounded by water on three sides. She was taking care of a granddaughter whose mom was at work when I arrived.

Maggie looks as though she has never had a care in the world—not with substance abuse and not with any of the concerns of business she must cope with every day as president of her own company. She has a beauty she carries lightly, as well as a refined air. Wearing a stylish sort of nubby turtleneck in a delicious strawberry hue and neat trousers, and looking poised and elegant, she was really a knockout with perfect classical features, quiet grace, and model posture. She also had at first that slight remoteness I've encountered in actresses—for at least partly the same reason, of training. She also had a way of talking straight without tailoring her story, which I remarked as impressive.

Before I left, when Maggie said she'd like to get together again sometime, I realized that having insight into her personality and hearing about her life was a privilege I personally would not have missed. I am positive she is a role model to many people my age and far younger and that her story that follows here will also inspire.

I had discovered that I could return home without traversing the formidable bridge a second time, but somehow after Maggie extolled the experience of crossing it daily, even of hesitating in the middle for joyous contemplation when there was traffic, I was sorry not to get the chance to drive over it with more confidence again.

---

## MAGGIE SHERMAN

There's no question in my mind that I'm an alcoholic. One of the earliest times I remember drinking was when I was fifteen. Being raised in the area of Maryland around Washington, D.C., you could drink at eighteen, so if you looked a little older in high school, you could get away with it in a lot of different places. After pom-pom practice in high school, I went down with a girl-friend to a place we knew would usually serve people underage. We had fake IDs. However, I made the tactical error of wearing my pom-pom uniform at the bar. Not a great decision. So I was taken out of the bar rather quickly, before we had any opportunity to make our transactions. My friend was gone so fast—she was driving—and I went to the holding tank at the police station.

I was a high school senior, and at that point I was too stupid to be terrified. There I was in my pom-pom uniform, with these prostitutes, and I'll never forget that one had on this pair of chartreuse toreadors and had hair that cascaded halfway down her back. I was staring at her and thinking, "How in the world did I get here?" I was also looking at myself in the pom-pom uniform as they took the laces out of my tennis shoes so I couldn't hang myself!

My dad was on a golf trip, so my mother came with a next-door neighbor to the police station to pick me up. Because I did not come from a drinking family or a permissive family, I figured it was all over—that I wouldn't get out of the house until I was thirty. We had definite rules, and being hauled off by the police was a big deal for me. I don't recall doing anything but smiling at my mom and going, "How the heck did this happen?" She just replied, "Don't you smile at me, young lady!" And we went home.

That was the first time I didn't get the clue to the game, because I was off and running in high school, and every time something chaotic happened, it was generally around me and alcohol. We went to parties, and because of where we lived, a lot of parties were on the water, and I, who gets very comfortable in water, got comfortable in water drunk. Once I went in and nobody ever saw me come out, and the whole hurrah was about me, people thinking I'd gone in and drowned. Again it was about booze.

I didn't know what I wanted to do after high school. I thought I wanted to teach speech in the theater, but right after graduation I went on the road and had a job as a secret shopper. This was when they still rang cash registers, and a team of us—a husband and wife, two other girls, and I—traveled around the country, going from city to city to each department store, where we would be disguised and go in and shop. We were taught how to shop to see if any of the employees were stealing money. It was a good experience. I grew up fast, and we had a good time. That trip was my first time drinking hard liquor. It's said if you can remember your first drink, that's significant, and I certainly do. It was an awakening. I had that first drink, and that's what I looked for from then on during that trip—when the guy was going to fix his pitcher of Bacardi cocktails and let us have a drink. It wasn't very much, but that got me started on hard liquor. We girls also would meet a couple of guys, and those occasions were lubricated by more hard liquor.

On that road trip I decided what to do, with the help of my mother, who sent me information on a college in Boston that specialized in theater. I really wanted to do that. So I left the road, auditioned at a Boston theater school, got in, and did a fair amount of partying while I was there. It was great. I loved it. I stayed in a dorm on the Fenway, and part of my drinking money was raised by dancing. We would climb out the window on the third floor of the dormitory, go down the fire escape into the alley, and go to a few of the jazz clubs that had go-go dancers. You could get a job as a go-go dancer and work a four-hour shift and be paid cash. Then you'd come back and climb up the fire escape to the dorm.

Go-go dancing was hard work! I used to make my drinking money doing it and remember racing up the fire escape to try and beat the housemother sometimes when she was coming back. Thank God she was old and I was fast at that point.

I did fairly well in school, though I did not set any records or light anything on fire. I was pretty good in theater so the academic part wasn't that important. I had a new source of drinking money by the last year of college when I discovered that I had a different kind of blood and so could sell my blood and get money. They wanted it as often as I could possibly manage to sell it in Boston, so I was getting my money that way and by working in bars. I worked in one of the older hotels, in the bar, and that was perfect. Overall I was learning how to work my alcoholic system. It's not that uncommon: all my jobs related to my freedom and ability to drink.

In retrospect I see how that progressed, how my ability to ferret out my opportunities to drink just increased. My last semester I made another really brilliant decision, that the world was better served if I worked with the Harvard underground against the war, and I dropped out of taking classes.

By that time I had no connection to anybody. By that stage of my drinking I had become so inward focused, so self-centered, that it didn't occur to me that that would disappoint anyone. It didn't occur to me that it would disappoint my parents, who paid for my college, especially my mom, who was working full time and gave me every dime she had to go toward a place for me to live. It just didn't connect because I didn't connect with anybody. Even in the early stages of my drinking, when I was fully functional, it did something to my insides. And today I relate that to becoming two-dimensional. It deflates your spiritual side so you move through life like a shadow. You're present and people see you, but you have no effect; you move through and people don't have any effect on you either. That began as soon as I picked up a drink as an alcoholic, and it kept up.

Having done theater all through college, I went from there to acting—didn't have trouble at all getting summer gigs and stayed on for winter at the theater where I was working. And I decided the last season that it was time to get married, so my best friend, a buddy from high school, and I decided to tie the knot.

Then I came back to Maryland, and lo and behold I found a job in a bar and was bar manager—surprise, surprise. I worked at two brand-new hotels. A security guy would go home, and a few of us would stay around after two o'clock, and we'd sort of wind down—being keeper of the keys suited me great. So I would close up in the middle of the night, drunk as anything, and then get on the beltway. I wasn't that familiar with the beltway, and I'd get out into the road, go into a blackout, and come out if it, and I never knew where I was. Again, my best thinking with the booze in me was a circle, to just keep drinking in a circle and you'll get to your exit. I would be driving around the beltway at three, four, five in the morning, waiting for my exit to come up a second time, because I had passed it.

And that would have just gone on, but I knew it wasn't the job to have as a newly married person, so I looked for more work and found a sales position at another hotel, in Rockville. And that started a whole career in hotel sales, not to mention it escalated my career in drinking very much, because that fit perfectly. When you're in hotel sales and you have to go out and entertain people, you have to show up for different industry functions in the evening. That really ruled me. It was another job made in heaven for an alcoholic, because it gave permission not to show up on time for work if you had been out entertaining people. Then it was a lot more acceptable than now to take clients out for drinks; a lot more people participated in that. You were expected to go to functions and that's what I did. So, needless to say, I drank my way through that marriage. It did not last.

The jobs built one upon the other in the hospitality industry. I never really got anywhere, but I was a great starter. A lot of us are wonderful starters, on fire and going to make all the difference in the world. But when it came to being able to be a worker bee and do things over and over, which you have to do in sales or marketing—you have to do repetitious, boring things, follow your leads, make phone calls, keep notes, and be very organized—I could not do that. In fact, I had no interest in doing that; it was boring and beneath me. I was a daily drinker at this point but still functional.

I was not a social drinker. I went home and drank until I passed out. One of the first things that I realized when I got sober was that there really was a difference between falling asleep and passing out! I had forgotten the distinction between the two.

During this time, I made a decent wage but never had any money left over. After I got into a program and into recovery, I looked into some boxes once and found old checkbooks from that period of my life. There wasn't a day that went by when I didn't write a check to a liquor store to buy my gallon of wine, quart of vodka, or whatever it was. I didn't realize it at the time, didn't get it. There were all kinds of opportunities, but being completely engaged in the disease of alcohol put a cloud on my ability to recognize reality, and to connect with other human beings; they were too much trouble, and it just let more and more air out of me. I got very flat, and my world got pretty small.

One evening, after getting drunk at an industry function, I got into an argument with a colleague. He left the party early, went straight to my apartment, and proceeded to cut up all my clothes, break all of my dishes, and trash the place. When I arrived at my apartment a few hours later, he was still there. And he was about six-foot-five and proceeded to beat the crap out of me.

I got away from him, and the next thing that I remember is after the police had gone, I was taken to the hospital. And sitting there getting stitched up a little bit, on the gurney in the hospital, going, "I wasn't raised this way. How in the world did I get here? How did this happen to me? It's not how I grew up." This was a wake-up call, and I didn't even get that! I didn't get right away that it had anything to do with alcohol.

My decision-making process continued to go from bad to worse. It was just never evident to me that the decisions I was making were so messed up. I lost my car several times when I lived in the apartment in D.C. I would park my car in a blackout, go up to my apartment, and have no clue what I had done with the car. And I'd be walking around the streets of D.C. looking for it the next morning before I could go to work.

And at work, I was a bit of a disaster. I had horrible hangovers. I had to give up drinking coffee to go to meetings in the morning, because my hand shook so badly that I couldn't drink anything without it being obvious. And it took me an extra-long time to apply mascara. But I didn't get the clues. When my hands were shaking so bad that I couldn't put my makeup on, it didn't occur to me that there might be something wrong. No, uh-uh. As I understand it today, that's what the disease does: it keeps going on.

At that point I was working in Georgetown, doing marketing. Again, it suited me, the timing suited me, mainly because it left me free to drink, and now I had a buddy to drink with. I met her someplace in Georgetown, and she happened to live in the same condominium complex as I did. She was married, and her husband was a recovering drug addict. She and I were drinking at my place one night and had a bottle of vodka. Both of us were sitting on the floor of the kitchen and sort of had the same epiphany at the same time. We looked at each other and said, "We are really bad alcoholics and we had better do something." And just sat on the kitchen floor and cried.

I think it was because we saw her husband in recovery that a message got through to us. For the first time in our lives, we were exposed to the idea that there was a possibility to recover (because he was a pretty bad drug addict and was actually doing pretty well). And so we knew where some help was, a group that we could affiliate with, and started going to recovery meetings. And it didn't work for me. The two of us would get all dressed up and go together; she stuck, I didn't. I went out for a couple of weeks, and I went to some meetings that had outpatients from St. Elizabeth's, and I looked around at some of the desperate cases there and said, "This is definitely not me." I knew I wasn't that bad at all. What I didn't know was that they were my future.

But after a couple of weeks I went back and began a process of recovery, and was one of the very fortunate ones that does not have to go out and test the waters yet again. People were put in my life, as was the twelve-step program, and the people that surrounded and supported me left me alone enough so that I could get my feet under me. By this I mean that I did not want anybody to care about me at that time: I didn't want you to talk about me, or be interested in me. The best I could do was go and sit and listen while other people talked. At that point I felt much better being that shadow on the wall that nobody paid attention to. And that's what I got; I got enough space.

Everybody that was with me somehow understood that I needed enough space to get myself into their circle. They were not allowed in my circle; my universe was closed to everybody. And that's the way my recovery took place—very gently, with a tremendous amount of support, exactly the right people at the right time. I got exactly what I needed—not particularly what I wanted, but what I needed, when and how I needed it. The people, places, things, opportunities, events—everything. And another friend of mine that shared the same experience was always fond of remarking about the serendipity of life, how everything fits together as it should. Certainly early on I could never relate to that, but the longer I have the opportunity to be a three-dimensional person, the more I see every single day the evidence of that serendipity, and of what I call God working in my life. I see that the right opportunities are put in front of me to take advantage of.

And that's also how I began my business, when I was in just the first year of recovery. I wish that I could say that I had a great five- or ten-year plan, or a crystal-clear vision, but the reason was that given the person I was becoming, I couldn't get along with the people I worked with. I couldn't be on time—that concept was too new to me—yet I needed to be honest about my failing. Until those first months in recovery, I never had to show up for a schedule or be that daily you-can-depend-on-me person. But when I began recovery, what happened was that I knew it was important for me not to lie, because I was told that. And when you can't lie and can't show up on time, it's a bad combination! It causes people to resent you when you say, "I overslept." Although I was working for a dear friend who was wonderful to me, I knew at some level that I had to get out before I was fired.

I had come up with an idea for a marketing business for people in the convention industry. So I took two weeks' vacation pay that I had earned and got it started.

It still amazes me today how quickly my business grew and changed during those early days. If I hadn't been given the people, support, and family that I had, I could not have gone ahead. And the message that I kept getting when I was putting this thing together, because it was scary trying to pay bills, do jobs, and structure the organization, was—I kept getting told—"Your history tells you that you can do this. Your history does not tell you that you're going to fail at working. You are capable of it, and now you're more awake, you're more than you were. You're not less than you were, you're just scared, and you're not used to being afraid." And I had to hear that message, from inside myself and others, almost daily sometimes when I was starting the business out. Because I didn't have a clue.

The other message I got was, "You're not supposed to know how to do everything. This is brand new. This is the first time you have ever tried to do this, period, much less sober. You're learning how to show up. You're learning how to be responsible. You're learning how to be self-sufficient through your own contributions." The last has become a big deal for me. It's the ground rules, the guide that I learned how to live by. And, if I didn't have that, I wouldn't have what I have today. I know that. There's no question in my mind at all.

And so you've got this business going, or your work, you've got your kids or your husband going on, but you also have this recovery thing going on, and that's the foundation, the block that you're going to stand on for building everything else. And if that goes away, everything that you built will just collapse. So I had to keep hearing that message every single day. Gradually, I got to trust new people enough to talk to them, and to let them a teeny bit into my life, and share a little bit of me and what was going on, and take off the mask. It was a very gradual process because I was a selfish, self-centered person.

When I came into recovery, the color of my wardrobe changed. For the first time in my life I bought things with color in them, whereas before that I wore all browns and blacks. And I went to dances. I never danced. I couldn't participate to start out with— only later. Somebody told me at a meeting in Georgetown that, if you're an alcoholic, you stop maturing emotionally the day that you pick up a drink, and you start again the day you put it down. That made a tremendous amount of sense to me. And the phases that I moved through in recovery didn't take as long day-to-day or year-to-year, but I recognize them—you can recognize changes in your behavior.

I especially recognized the discomfort I felt in forming relationships. And the reason was that I didn't do it before. My booze did it. So I was learning to form all kinds of new relationships and have experiences that were new to me. Because that part of me hadn't grown up. I relate to the reality of this almost as though I let my soul off the hook when I was fifteen years old and didn't invite it back in until I was thirty-six. So there's a real big gap there, of any soul growth, of spiritual maturing, and the soul kind of withers up.

A soul needs to be fed, and I was very fortunate to be fed also in the recovery program. That part of me woke up, which was another key to being able to do what I was able to do in my work life. The business that I started came into operation so typically, at a kitchen table; however, I was bad at it initially, because I lacked discipline. I would sit at the kitchen table and do some work, and get up and go make soup. And I would sit down and do some work, and get up and go make coffee. And I would get down to work, and jump up and do the wash, make my bed, and so forth. And I thought, "This is not working for me. I cannot do this at home. I'm just not that kind of person. I need people around me."

So, I went to a meeting one day and ran into a gentleman who was able to get me an entire suite of offices in downtown D.C. for $300 a month. It was as if he got plopped down next to me via serendipity or my higher power. How much more of a gift can you get? So I was able to hire a person, and she came, because the timing was right for her; she was getting ready to retire early from a transportation company. My mother also came to work with me. So it began with three of us. I had an office and an IBM Selectric, and that was it. And recovery, and people in recovery. And that was how I was handed exactly what I needed when I needed it. The first year I was able to pay all of my bills. And to this day I don't know why—I think somebody vouched for me—but a bank gave me a loan. That kept me going for another year.

Everything from then on kept growing, including me. I needed to be in Washington for the time that I was there, because I met with the other people in recovery every day—at least twice a day for about six years. That's what I needed to stay grounded and come back to life and be able to do all I did. I needed to listen to other people. It's not that I was smart and knew what I was doing, because often I didn't. All I knew how to do was show up, and listen, and start learning to take some instructions. And the other part that was a benchmark for me is that I learned how to share. I learned how to give what I learned back to other people eventually. And that was tremendously valuable to me, to learn that the philosophy, the twelve steps, that tell you that in order to keep it you have to give it away, actually worked. And I felt that inside myself. I always used to talk to others about not being able to relate emotionally to what I knew to be true. I said, "I get it up here but I can't get it below the neck."

Because the feelings had gone away. It was very important when I was drinking not to feel much. So the ability to feel other things for other people came into my life and it was amazing. Waking up to feeling really cool things about people, like appreciation and joy and what it was like to love, was like Christmas. To recognize my mom (my father died while I was still drinking) stunned me: what had been given so freely in my life that I never sensed. That's pretty strong as far as awakenings go, but part of a wonderful process.

I got married during this process—that's an important part of it—to someone who was also in recovery. We stayed in Washington, D.C., moved around a little, which afforded me the opportunity to stay close to that whole community of people, which was really important—I required it then. And I seem to have been handed things on a silver platter sometimes in recovery, regarding my business in particular. It kept growing. It got really expensive downtown, and parking was expensive, and I drove by a building that was for sale in Maryland, an office condominium. I ended up being able to buy that for less than we were able to park in Washington, D.C. And it saved everybody that I had working for me at the time, which was four people.

So I left downtown Washington, D.C., with the business, and my husband and I moved to Maryland, and I got established with another group of people in recovery, which again was very important. I became closer to other women, and I was now giving back on a more consistent level to others in recovery.

The business continued to grow beyond my wildest dreams—everything did. The going from a condo that my mother helped me buy to where I live in a spacious house by the sea today is a miracle to me. I do not understand fully how I got here! And I guess that's why it's a little hard to talk about. There are no steps one, two, three, which are prescribed to be able to do what I was able to do. My opinion is that for me, my success in business derives from the fact that in my recovery I am able to recognize gifts when they are presented to me. A gift of people that have been with me a long time or of a person who only worked for a year or two and then had to move on. It's being grateful. It's a profound feeling that I am not the one responsible for where I sit today. And that is so different a feeling than what I had inside me when I was drinking that I can scarcely believe it.

I get up and go to work every day. I never did anything consistently when I was drinking. I've gotten up and gone to work and been consistent and learned discipline every day for twenty-four years.

I didn't do that. There was an opportunity that was given to me to grow something on a strong foundation and not just keep chasing my tail.

And it grew. I have sixty-five full-time employees and probably another sixty-five who, because of the kind of work that we do, work part-time. And I see lives that are affected. Because of the recovery process I was offered, it's as if I see a huge tree, like a family tree, that came out of the bounty I have experienced, that touches hundreds of people, because I was given what I needed when I needed it and was able to stay away from alcohol and grow as a human being. And that just blows my mind. It's amazing to be sitting here and to be available to my family. Everything's not always hunky-dory. It's not always a breeze at work or in my personal life, but I show up today. I do the things I'm supposed to do when I'm supposed to do them, for the most part, and I have genuine feelings of joy and appreciation when I see other people able to grow as a result of anything—it doesn't have to be recovery, just human beings growing.

Something I always get a kick out of, and that helps me stay on the right track in business, is my take on failure. The people who work for me used to laugh at my optimism when things seem down, but not now because they subscribe to the same philosophy, which is that whenever we don't get a job, or something doesn't come to us that we want, the belief is that it wasn't supposed to happen that way. Now all we have to do is wait and see why. That's the only thing that I wait for anymore; I wait for the lesson.

You know, not waiting to be rescued but waiting instead for the lesson is a huge, important shift. Evidence keeps presenting itself: "Oh, that's why we didn't get that piece of work." Or, "That's why I had to go away during that period of time when I thought I should be home." This is something I've been able to share with some of the women who are in my life now. It helps make sense of everything. If I have a belief in my God, or higher power, and a belief that I am here to learn lessons and do the best I can with what I have, then everything makes sense. I don't like everything clarity brings, not by a long shot, but everything makes sense to me. I say to myself, "Whose lesson is this anyway?"

I used to presume that they were all *my* lessons but kind of came to the conclusion, "You know what? They aren't all mine, I just get put in sometimes and am just this little piece. Someone else needs to be someplace so they can have this lesson, so I need to get out of the picture." As an alcoholic, learning that it's not all about me is a big lesson.

Nothing is lost, so, second-guessing the "what if"—What if I wasn't an alcoholic? What if I'm not who I was when I was born? What if my dad didn't die then?—is pointless. What counts is what is, because that's our school. You can feel in your bones when you learn something, and that's amazing.

When I was starting out in my business, which is a very male-dominated business, I went through a long period where I felt I really wasn't taken seriously, and I resented having to prove myself every time I walked into somebody's office. A young man, too, has to pay his dues, yet I think this is more the case with a woman. And I went through a lot of years where I was pissed because I didn't want to have to prove myself because I was a female in a business with men mostly twenty years my senior. Having a tremendous support group and a place to go to talk about my hopes and fears helped me not to panic. Because the other part of who was dealing with the hidebound attitudes was an alcoholic, and the first thing that alcoholics want to do when they get uncomfortable is go back to that place of comfort. And that place of comfort is inside a bottle.

That's why we stick together, and that's why many of us who have just been able to keep going accomplish it with tremendous support. The one thing you do not have to do is drink. You can be rude, abrasive, fearful, anything you want to be, but you can't pick up a drink, because if you pick up a drink, then your choices about who you are and the life you will lead go away. You no longer have a choice of how you are going to react. It just leaks out over everybody; it comes out with the booze. So I heard that loud and clear.

Some people begin recovery with an idea of, "Oh, I wasn't that bad." Very early on I was so lucky that I got it. At one point I remarked, "I wasn't that bad—I could probably go out and drink for another five or ten years." Looking at me as if I was crazy, a woman who has since passed from multiple sclerosis sort of drew herself up and said, "Yes, my dear, but you'll never know if you'll get back in or not."

For some reason, at that moment I understood what I was going to hear for many years after that, about people who go in and out of sobriety. It was as if I got the massage before the crick in my neck. It has stuck with me so clearly that there is a line with addiction that you can cross but that you can't then get back over. No matter how hard you want to. So why would I want to find out where that line is? I have had too many gifts given to me in this lifetime to even want to know if I'm close to that line. It's hardly worth it. So I was fortunate in that lesson.

It's very important for us as women to recognize that we've had things going on in our systems that we have not been paying attention to. The pain we drank to is unfamiliar—such as the PMS symptoms. So all of a sudden we get emotions that are flooding us because we are fully functioning for the first time without taking the substance that dulled us. Now we're just experiencing what most women learn how to do themselves all along.

If you've never experienced pain, and all of a sudden you get feeling—the marking time is over. And if someone pricks you with a pin you think you've been hit by a tractor. That's what the emotions feel like when you start recovering. You feel like a teenager dealing with relationships, but you do catch up fast. I've found the most healing part of the recovery, that kind of greases the way, is the spiritual side.

Could I have had a more even path? Do I have to have the struggles? In one way or another I believe you do. I believe that's why we are here. And I believe exactly what they told me in my recovery program, that you never get more than you can handle. I believe that we agree to what we came for here. And that sometimes it works out and sometimes it's too hard. Because I don't think that we're a lot different on the other side than we are here. Underneath our daily lives, excitement vibrates all the time, because our spirits rest and yearn underneath our daily routines. Sometimes we bite off more than we can chew. For some people, the anxiety of that is more painful than they are prepared to deal with here. That is a lesson in itself.

# 7

# William Cope Moyers

*No one feels good at four in the morning.*
*If ants feel good at four in the morning*
*three cheers for the ants. And let five o'clock come*
*if we're to go on living.*

—Wislawa Szymborska, "Four in the Morning"

I t was with no small amount of apprehension that I flew off to San Diego, California, to interview William Cope Moyers. Traveling all the way from my home in Connecticut seemed like a huge effort just to meet with someone I could have spoken with on the phone, but my intuition told me it would be worth it—that to get him to take this project seriously, I needed to meet him face-to-face. I knew, for instance, that Moyers has been interviewed dozens of times and is constantly speaking on the lecture circuit and that unless I had a chance to look him in the eye and explain the purpose of my book, he might treat my interview request as simply another day at the office.

Upon arriving at the hotel/mini-resort/conference center where Moyers was scheduled to speak that night, I checked in and called his room. No one answered, so I headed down to the lobby to snoop around. It was raining like crazy that afternoon, but the first person I encountered when I got out of the elevator was a guy who had obviously just come in from a run. Shorts, a soaked-through T-shirt, and squishy running shoes were a good clue. I thought I recognized him to be Moyers, but since we had never met before I wasn't sure, so I let him enter the elevator without asking. A minute later I called his room again and he quickly answered.

After sharing a few quick observations about our running prowess (I, too, have pounded the pavements for many years), we agreed to meet in the hotel restaurant where this interview was conducted. What I remember most about the experience was how focused he is and how easily he opens up and shares his story, his emotional pain, and, most important, his newfound life in recovery.

## WILLIAM COPE MOYERS

My name is William Cope Moyers, and I use my full name because my family, and people who met me before I went into recovery, know me by my middle name. My byline as a journalist is Cope Moyers, and having that middle name was perfect for a practicing alcoholic, like I wasn't able to cope with life very well. Later on in life, I started using the name William as part of my second chance.

I was born in 1959, in Fort Worth, Texas. My father, when I was born, was an ordained Southern Baptist minister; my mother was a home economist. My father was at theology school at Southwestern Theology Seminary in Fort Worth. Both my parents have deep roots in Texas, so I'm a child of the South, which I think is important for a lot of reasons.

The Kennedy assassination in 1963 was a huge moment in American history and also profoundly affected our family life.

My father was heavily involved in politics by then. He started out working as a summer intern for President Lyndon B. Johnson and became heavily involved in Johnson's campaigns. My father was first appointed as associate director of public affairs for the newly created Peace Corps in 1961 and served as deputy director from 1962 to 1963. When Johnson took office after the Kennedy assassination, he became a special assistant to Johnson, serving from 1963 to 1967.

So we moved to Washington, D.C., and my father worked in the White House. I remember trips on Air Force One, Easter egg hunts on the south lawn of the White House, the president coming over for dinner, and a lot of fancy stuff. I remember from an early age, and I think it was relevant to what would happen to me later on, that I began to get this sense that I wasn't good enough and I needed to be "better than." My life on the outside was perfect, and I was something less than that on the inside, and I did not like the way I felt about that. I wasn't noteworthy like all of the people who worked with my dad. I had what I've come to call a hole in my soul.

For me it's underneath my rib cage on the left side of my gut that aches with a sense of imperfection. It aches with a sense that I'm not good enough, that I need to be better than, and it aches with a sense of restlessness, irritability, and discontent. Long before I took a drink or a drug, I was painfully aware that I wasn't good enough and that I didn't fit in.

This hole in the soul has been with me from a very early age. I remember when I was in kindergarten, in northern Virginia (during the time when my father was in the White House), the principal from my elementary school called my parents and said, "Mr. and Mrs. Moyers, your son is giving away his silver dollar collection on the school playground."

That's when silver dollars were made out of real silver! And I was giving away my collection and didn't know why I was doing that. With the benefit of hindsight in recovery, I've been able to look back and realize I was trying to soothe the hole in my soul by giving others something that would result in their giving me adoration and love. When I would give away my coins on the playground, the other kids were giving back what I needed to medicate or soothe this hole in my soul.

Another time, when I was in first or second grade, I went to school with a big bandage on my head. There was nothing wrong with me, but all my classmates flocked around me to see what was wrong. "What happened?" I made up some story—I don't even remember what it was, it didn't matter. When I got sympathy from the other kids, it soothed that hole. Never mind that the next day I went back to school without the bandage on my head and everybody came up to me and said, "You've been miraculously healed."

I got the same result with frequency. I got all the attention I sought. That's how I lived my life. It's very difficult, the life of perfectionism in the body of a human being.

The other thing was that I was raised with the very keen sense of a power greater than myself, God. God was great, God was good, and we thanked God for our food every night at the dinner table. Amen. That was our prayer. The God of my understanding was a big powerful man with a long beard and flowing white robes, and He could do anything.

But in 1971 the God of my understanding died. I was in Red River, New Mexico. I was twelve years old. I was with my mother, father, sister, and brother. I witnessed the death of a family that got struck and killed by lightning while sitting underneath a tree. A whole family. That day—July 18, 1971—was the day that my faith died. This moment is really relevant to the second chance I'll talk about later. I had always believed that God was great and God was good. But how could that be? In his greatness had He created a lightning bolt that came out of the clouds and touched one of three million trees in a forest and directed that tree to strike down and kill a family underneath it? On the other hand, if He hadn't directed this to happen, why if His power was so great couldn't He stop it from happening? Either way, I could not answer. But neither option sat well with me. And so my faith died.

I faked belief for a long time, but my faith had died. I was so moved by that experience, and so desperate to get my faith back, that two weeks after I witnessed it, I had my father baptize me in this Southern Baptist Church in a small Texas town where my mother grew up. Where my grandparents were deacons in the church. It was the old-style baptism where they lower you down in the water and bring you back. I wanted the baptism to wash me clean of my doubt. That was on August 1, 1971 (I still have that certificate hanging up in my home office).

It didn't work. So I've got two strikes against me: a hole in my soul that aches with a sense of imperfection and a faith that had died. Lo and behold, the third element of the galloping trio of alcoholic danger: my brain, which processes alcohol differently than 90 percent of the people in this country.

When I was fifteen years old I smoked marijuana for the first time. This was the first mood- or mind-altering substance I ever used. I was in about the tenth grade, and that marijuana instantly did for me what I could not do for myself. It made me feel great, but it also flipped on a light switch in my brain, which I could not turn off on my own, because I have that kind of brain. I was off to the races. I developed that baffling inability to "just say no." I started smoking marijuana regularly—not a lot, but enough. I started drinking alcohol at the legal age of eighteen. My friends drank in college and used hard drugs, and so did I.

In August 1988 neither drugs nor alcohol was working for me anymore, and I smoked crack cocaine for the first time. That was during the great crack epidemic on the East Coast in the late eighties. I smoked crack and it knocked me to my knees. Literally. And

I thought, "This is it, this is the answer." Just a short year after that, I found myself holed up in a crack house on the corner of 104th and Central Park West. A New York City crack house.

The hideous thing about it is that all during the 1980s, I was married to my high school sweetheart, who had no clue about my drug and alcohol use. On August 6, 1989, I was checked into St. Vincent's Hospital in New York City for being a crazy person. My wife took me there and they asked her, "What is your husband here for?" She told them, "I think he has a short-term alcohol problem." And then they called me into the intake room and said, "Mr. Moyers, what are you here for?" I replied, "I have a long-term cocaine problem." Those two things didn't match up, so I had to go out into the hallway and tell my wife, and she collapsed on the floor. The whole time she had been married to me, I was in love with somebody else. Cocaine. And of course, relationships are built on trust, and there's no trust if you're using, so the marriage died. Just like that. That day. It just died.

So I spent three weeks in the psych ward in New York City, and then I was shipped to Hazelden. I would be in treatment four times over the next five years, between 1989 and 1994.

In the early nineties, I went to work as a journalist at CNN. I married the woman I'm with now, Allison. We met in early recovery in St. Paul, Minnesota. We were both getting sober. We moved to Atlanta, I got a really good job, and we had two babies immediately. We were in our early thirties, and I managed to stay sober for the next three years. Then in 1994 I relapsed. I relapsed because I treated my recovery like I treated taking out the garbage. Maybe once a week. Sort of an afterthought. An obligation that I could work around. I didn't become an alcoholic and a drug addict. My addiction to alcohol and drugs became me. Every cell in my body. And if I didn't steward it and take care of myself, it was going to get me. And it did. It got me.

When I went to treatment in the summer of 1994, I did so mainly to ward off the threat by CNN that I would be fired if I didn't go. In other words, I complied but did not surrender. And doing anything on my terms was risky, as I soon discovered again. I managed to stay sober for about sixty-six days after that, but soon the illness caught up with me and overtook me again. When I went back to the crack house in October of '94, I went there to die, not to get high, because I had been overwhelmed with it all. I could not live anymore with this hole in my soul. I wasn't working the steps of my program, drugs weren't working anymore, and I was done. I was finished. It was a Sunday afternoon. I said good-bye to Allison and the baby boys, and I went off to the crack house.

Then, on October 12, I was delivered, as all of us in recovery are. I was at this terrible place in the inner city of Atlanta, smoking crack, but it wasn't working. I stuck out there like a sore thumb. I had money in my pocket and I was a white guy. Had I not had money, they would have killed me. I had been missing for four or five days. CNN didn't know where I was; my wife didn't know where I was. My dad and mom came to Atlanta to look for me. The CEO of CNN—Ted Turner's right-hand man in the organization and former publisher of the *L.A. Times*—Tom Johnson (whom my son Thomas is named for), actually had the police, and even cab drivers, out looking for me.

My father and mother had raised me to be a resilient young man. They said to me, "Son, if you put your mind to it, if you work hard, and if you have a little bit of luck, you can do anything." I had had a successful career as a newspaper reporter and a journalist working at CNN. All of a sudden, as I was sitting in that crack house, smoking crack, I had this question pop into my head: "Now what?" I could not give an answer.

And my second chance began right then. Why? Because I got up off the floor of that crack house, through no power of my own, and I walked out. Past all the other hopeless and helpless souls who were in there. Who were no different than I, except for two things: one was the color of their skin, and two, they probably weren't lucky enough to get a second chance. They didn't have money; they didn't have a support network, an employer, a wife; they didn't have a structure in their lives. And I did have those things. It wasn't all about me; in fact, I was delivered despite me. I had a disease that wanted me dead. But I went into treatment in October of '94, and I've been clean and sober ever since.

So what's the relevance of this second chance thing? Well, I've been chasing my father's shadow since I was conscious. That's part of why I have the hole in my soul. My father's not the reason why, but I think I pulsated with the pain of not being as good as he was. I didn't deserve to be flying on Air Force One, or having the president invite me to the White House, or living in a nice home, or being loved. I didn't feel like I deserved any of that. In part because of the adulation many people have for my father, despite his faults, which I'm keenly aware of.

That's pretty perverse. Because I couldn't feel good about myself unless I felt I measured up. What worse way to exacerbate my problems than to try and become my father? It's like holding on to a hot poker. It's burning, but you still hold on. I kept running from my shadow, but you know how far we get—not far. It's always there. In this case it was the shadow of my imperfection, which in part was the shadow cast by the brilliant sun of my father's fame.

When I went into treatment in the fall of '94 I went to a place called Ridgeview Institute, which is where CNN sent a lot of people. While in treatment there I broke my foot playing volley-ball. Since Ridgeview was kind of set up like a college campus, getting around with a broken foot became problematic. It was the first time in my life I truly had to ask for help. And not to be ashamed. That experience sort of softened me up for these teachable moments in treatment. That's why treatment worked. I stayed there for a hundred days.

One day at Ridgeview, I'm lying in my bed, feeling sorry for myself because of my broken foot, in a little bit of pain, at the treatment center. I'd been sober three or four weeks maybe, and I hear this whisper in my ear: "St. Paul." It was out loud. There was no one in the room, but I heard the words "St. Paul." I did not know the story of St. Paul the saint, so I thought that whoever was whispering that in my ear was telling me to go to St. Paul, Minnesota, where I had been in treatment at Hazelden and where I had also lived in a halfway house.

St. Paul is a really good town for recovery people. There are thousands of us living there. You can move to St. Paul and you don't have to explain to a prospective employer what that hole is in your résumé. "What do you mean, you used to be a big-time journalist and reporter in New York, and now you are out here in St. Paul trying to get this job at a bookstore?" "Well, I just finished treatment at Hazelden." "Oh, OK. You go over there and start working."

So anyway, I hear this whisper of "St. Paul," and I know it sounds hokey, but I knew if I wanted to stay sober, I had to go to any lengths, and any lengths for me meant trusting the process. The answer wasn't St. Paul. That was just the next step.

It was about that time that my belief in God, which had been killed by that lightning strike, came back to me, but in a different way. As a kid, I had always believed in God, and then he died for me in 1971. In 1994 it became clear to me that this wasn't about just believing in God, it was about trusting in God. That God can do for me what I can't do for myself. It was a huge shift from trying to believe in this God to trusting that whatever that power is, it will lead me to where I need to go. And so, as an impulsive type, a personality instead of leaving that bed, on my broken foot, yelling,

"I've been saved, and I'm going to St. Paul." Though I had to stay in treatment for the full 100 days, my mind had been made up. I was going to St. Paul.

When I got out of treatment, I told my wife, "We've got to move to St. Paul, Minnesota." She said, "Why? To do what?" And I said, "I don't know." Again she said, "Why?" And I said, "Because we have to."

So I went back to the CEO of CNN, Tom Johnson, a great man, not to mention a big, powerful guy, and said, "Tom, I'm leaving CNN." He leaned over his big desk and said to me, "Are you crazy? You're sober, you're doing great, you have a tremendous career here. Are you crazy?" To which I replied, "Maybe."

Tom was born in Macon, Georgia. He's ten years younger than my father. My father took Tom, this kid, under his wing and was his mentor at the White House. And, like my father, Tom (a child of the Great Depression) was from a dirt-poor family. He believed that you would never leave a job unless you had a job. "You just don't do that." But here I was, leaving this career and tremendous job, where I made really good money, with a wife who did not work outside the home and two hungry boys, to go back to St. Paul, Minnesota. Why? Because I had to go to any lengths.

And so we sold our house in Atlanta, made a little money on the deal, and packed up our stuff and moved back to St. Paul. A lot of people think I moved to St. Paul to work at Hazelden. But I didn't start working there until a year later. I moved to St. Paul because that's what I had to do. I didn't know what was going to happen. I didn't return there expecting anything. I went because that's what I had to do. No plan. My family and I settled in there and we said, "Now what?"

I was trying to start a little communications business. Until I found out what I could do, I became a communications consultant. Unfortunately, there was more money going out than coming in. I was making a fraction of what I was making at CNN just a couple of months before. Though it wasn't working out financially, I still had clarity. I think that when we're in pain, when things are really hard, is when we have this clarity. The clarity was awareness of my world. I had been living in Minnesota for five or six months, looking for potential clients for my new business in the classified ads every week. (I never used to look at the classifieds before because I always had good jobs. I was always very employable, very successful.) If I see that the 3M Company is looking for a communications writer, I'm going to tell them they don't need to hire a writer, they need to hire a consultant.

But there I was reading the *Minneapolis Star-Tribune* classifieds on Sunday, November 19, 1995. And there it was: "Wanted. Public Policy Specialist. Hazelden Foundation." It was as if somebody had picked up a glass of water and thrown it in my face.

I wasn't sure if I was right for the job, so I prayed about it. This job became that real second chance I wasn't even looking for. And I started working there. It was Leap Day, February 29, 1996, when I went to work as a public policy specialist at the Hazelden Foundation. I knew nothing about public policy. Particularly as it related to the addictions field. Hazelden took a chance and hired me, even though there were other people who were far more qualified, including the sons of some key politicians in the state of Minnesota. I took this job working at Hazelden earning $40,000 a year, at the age of thirty-seven. There's nothing wrong with $40,000 a year, but when you were previously making six figures, and you have a wife and two kids, and when you were once on the fast track to becoming a senior correspondent or key manager in a for-profit company, it's pretty humbling. But I did it because it was the right thing to do. I didn't do it for altruistic reasons. I did it because it was just the right thing to do. It had my name on it.

My first day on the job was in Washington, D.C. I remember the plane coming down over the Potomac River, and I'm thinking, "What the hell am I doing? I've never been to Washington, except as 'the son of' or as a tourist. What is this about? What am I supposed to do?"

I learned a lot that first year. I couldn't believe how little I knew before then. At age thirty-seven, with a good career behind me, I knew nothing. Barry McCaffrey was the U.S. drug czar at the time, under Bill Clinton. He had been a four-star general and had been to Bosnia during its war and also to Vietnam. This was 1997. It was really the turning point for me, and the event that launched me into the fourth dimension of my existence. I stood up in the meeting we were having and I said, "General McCaffrey, why is the drug policy in this country so divorced from reality?"

The drug policy in this country under Clinton was basically the same as it was before him under George Bush and Ronald Reagan—and it was largely ineffective. The lion's share of the money got spent on law enforcement and interdiction, with very little money left over for what really works, including recovery and introducing addicts to a new way of life.

So, though my second chance was really grounded in my going to Hazelden, the piece that became hugely relevant to my existence today, in this career I have, was when I asked Barry McCaffrey that question. We were in a ballroom of a hotel in Washington. He was twenty feet away from me—a four-star general, drug czar of the United States—and I'm asking this question to this guy. I mean, who am I to be asking the guy this question?

Barry McCaffrey knew that I was in recovery. I don't know how he knew that, but he wagged his finger at me and said, "William, the problem is that you are invisible." I thought to myself, "Wait a minute. He saw me. What does he mean?" And then I knew right what he meant: the problem is that we addicts in recovery are invisible. He went on to say that if you want to change drug policy, you have to stand up and speak out and put a face on recovery so that policy makers can see that treatment works and recovery is possible. Tell them, "Here we are, and it looks like us."

That was the day I realized I needed to become public as a recovering person. It was easy for me because I was working for a treatment center. I wouldn't lose my job over going public. It was right after that when I was at a Rotary Club meeting in St. Paul, giving my first speech about being a person in recovery. Since then I've given maybe two thousand speeches and presentations to churches, in the White House, to civic groups, and on major TV shows.

For that Rotary Club meeting, I wrote this brilliant speech about the disease of addiction and the terrible toll it takes and the diminished productivity in the workplace, and all of that. Speaking at a Rotary meeting is often impossible. You speak right after lunch to a bunch of old white men, and they're exhausted from eating that big roast chicken lunch. Either that or they don't care about what you have to say and just want to get the hell out of there.

So I got up there that day and I gave that speech: "I'm here today as a public policy specialist, and I'm going to talk to you about drug addiction." I looked out over the audience of about 150 or so and saw that some were trying to sneak out the rear, others were eating their dessert, and the rest were nodding off. I realized, "I'm losing these guys!" So I took my talk and I put it aside and said, "Let me tell you a real story. I'm a drug addict and an alcoholic." And you should have seen the room. It was amazing. "Not you, not the son of Bill Moyers, not an official at Hazelden, not the nice guy we all know, or the guy who's on the board of a bank in St. Paul. You can't be one of those drunks."

It was amazing. Barry McCaffrey saying "you're invisible" and me putting a face on the issue from my own life and experience— that was the transforming moment. It wasn't just one thing that happened; it was a series of things. The whisper "St. Paul," to the "Now what," which I couldn't answer, to the classifieds, to praying about it all, to McCaffrey. And then my life took off. You have to be careful how you share your story in public. I never talk about my using experiences in any way that people can construe it as having fun or that they can glamorize. Never. But I also don't talk about it in all the sordid details because that is not appropriate. I don't talk about it in public the same way that I talk about it at a recovery meeting.

I was actually pretty good, because being a journalist I knew how to write and I knew the power of language, and my father had taught me to be a good speaker by getting me to speak at churches and things like that. I never really had done public speaking, but I just knew how to do it. My father's very eloquent and my mother, too. So I had the gift of communication, and I harnessed that into a personal passion for helping the still-suffering alcoholics and this mission. I could never have scripted all this. I think it was just the confluence of these events in my life. You know that line about, "Coincidences are God's way of remaining anonymous." How else can I explain why my life worked out this way? I'm not sure I would have come out the other side like I have had I not experienced the death of that family. Or my near death. I thank God every day. Every night when I go to bed I say, "Thanks, God. Thanks a lot." You know, I've had some bad days during the last two years, but my worst day sober is better than my best day drunk.

# 8

# Peter Jaquith

*"If you know what a conflict goes on in the business*
*mind, when the business mind is divided between*
*good-natured impulse and business appearances, you*
*would be amused, Mr. Darnay." Mr. Lorry reddened,*
*and said, warmly, "You have mentioned that before,*
*sir. We men of business, who serve a House, are not*
*our own masters. We have to think of the House more*
*than ourselves."*

—CHARLES DICKENS, *A TALE OF TWO CITIES*

The plot of Evelyn Waugh's *Brideshead Revisited*, a classic fiction of British upper-class life, hinges on one moment when Sebastian Flyte, an Oxford bad boy who becomes a naughty roué, pretends to go on a fox hunt from his castle, when he is really giving his family the slip so he can stop at the village pub and get inebriated. Sebastian gets the money for his spree from his best friend, Charles. Lady Flyte banishes Charles from the house for it; but on her deathbed she apologizes to him. It's understood that unless the person is ready to change, denying him the money or access to his poison is futile.

Peter Jaquith drank heavily during his impressive career as corporate lawyer and investment banker. A man with a great degree of lucidity but also caustic humor, he wrote for his Dartmouth alumni magazine in the spring of 2006 that *D* for him meant not only Dartmouth but Denial of the substance abuse problem he had had ever since college days.

Could someone have protected him or set him straight? Jaquith knows others saw him as arrogant and bullish, and after losing his career to his drug habit he has come back a far happier individual sober. For him being sober has been a revelation where he can love his family and shed the arrogance that had been so ingrained.

---

# PETER JAQUITH

I grew up in the small New England town of Clinton, Massachusetts, a community of about twelve thousand residents. My father was an attorney and a special justice of the district court, and my mother was a housewife. She had two daughters and a son—she had no other career. Through my sophomore year in high school, I went to the public schools, at which point my parents decided to remove me from bad influences in the community, among my peers, and that had to do more with finding me in the pool hall than anything pertaining to substance abuse. And so my parents paraded me around the various prep schools in the area to see if I could be removed to a private school for the last two years of high school.

As it turned out, I was accepted at Phillips Academy in Andover, Massachusetts. I did not have to repeat a year and graduated in two years from Phillips Academy. While there I was introduced by my peers to hard alcohol. Prior to that I just had exposure to beer, which I had consumed to the point of inebriation a few times.

So it was on a trip to Yale University where the Andover track team was competing against the freshman team of Yale when I was introduced to hard alcohol. It was a result of that trip that I found myself totally drunk on a Saturday night. I had my first blackout and found myself coming to in a cold shower with all my clothes on and two of my fellow track mates holding me up. That's all I remember of that incident, and it strangely didn't deter me from pursuing alcohol. In my senior year at Andover, I used to go down to the alumni house on campus where liquor was available. There was a supply in-house, which I would steal and take back to my room. Of course, it wasn't permitted, so I had to find a spot in the room to keep it from being discovered during an inspection. I managed to find a loose chair rail in the wall, and behind the chair rail I could access the inner recesses of the wall without making a mark. I used to keep my stolen liquor in there. I'd hang it by a string on a nail; I had access to it at will.

That was my exposure to alcohol at the beginning. And I went from Andover to Dartmouth College and became a full-blown alcoholic in college. There was a lot of unimpeded heavy drinking at Dartmouth; I just took it to an extreme. I partied all the time. I used to give a speech on the weekends in my fraternity to the woman with the biggest breasts who came to one of our parties. She would have a little pin put on her chest as an award, and I would get up and make a speech. It was called the Alexander P. Grumby Award, and they'd come from all over campus to hear this award speech I'd give every weekend. That speaks pretty much for my level of maturity at the time.

I did not do my schoolwork but managed to maintain a barely passing average. Although I flunked a couple of courses, I was able to hang on and get my first two years of college in before I was able to depart because of an incident that occurred in the spring of my sophomore year. I was on scholarship at Dartmouth, and one of the requirements was that the scholarship people had to stay at school after final exams to work during the graduation period serving food and drinks to the alumni and the parents of the graduating class. There would be liquor tents set up on campus. We would be asked to tend bar and monitor supplies in those tents. One evening late I had to relieve myself and chose to do so near a bush on the campus, on the outside of a dormitory wall, and a policeman came along and arrested me. I got into a shouting match with him, and when I got home after the duty was completed, about a week later, I had a letter in the mail advising me that I would not be welcome back to the school in the fall and that I had to take a two-year sabbatical. It was suggested that I get a job and possibly go into the military. In those days every male my age was subject to the draft, and it was likely that a young man not in school would be called to serve two years in the military.

Because of that letter I chose to volunteer for the draft and was inducted into the U.S. Army in September 1956, which was the year after my sophomore year at Dartmouth. I was sent to boot camp at Fort Dix and then to Fort Chaffee in Arkansas. Sixteen weeks of boot camp and then I was shipped over to Hawaii, where I spent the rest of my service. I managed to get an early departure from the Army—three months earlier than my two-year requirement—so that I could return to school. I had written to Dartmouth, and they accepted me back in the fall. I only had to complete a course in summer school to meet the requirements of going into my junior year, so I spent the summer taking Russian history at Harvard Summer School for the appropriate credits.

In my junior year at Dartmouth, of course, my prior behavior became my current behavior and I partied again. And in the spring of my junior year my fraternity brothers and I went to Smith College on a weekday—we hitchhiked down there because none of us had a car—and spent the afternoon and evening with a couple of young ladies at Smith, drinking in a local Northampton pub. We took them back to Smith at midnight. Realizing that we had no way to get home, we decided to spend the remainder of the evening at a fraternity at Amherst College, which was adjacent to Smith in the next town.

We hitchhiked over there and walked on campus, where I had a friend in the DEKE fraternity house who had given me a standing invitation to spend the night if I were ever unable to get a ride back to Dartmouth. When we got to the house it was totally dark and locked. I said to my companion, "We'll just break in this window and go in, and since my friend has given me this invitation, I'll let him know we're responsible for the window. He'll send a bill, and we'll send him the money to repair it."

So in we went. There were no lights anywhere. You couldn't see anything, and we didn't turn any lights on going in: we just went up the stairs. By the time we got to the third floor where the bedrooms were, I opened the door and there was this white-haired lady asleep in her bed. So I turned to my friend and said, "We're in the wrong house." Whereupon we started to leave, and he dropped his beer bottle on the wooden staircase.

This aroused the entire household, and the ladies got up—there were two of them living in the house, I guess. Anyway, we scrambled through that hole in the window and I managed to slice my leg on a shard of glass. I said we would have to go to the emergency room. My leg was killing me; it was bleeding like a stuck pig. My friend drove me to the hospital, where they stitched up my leg. It was there that we met our fate, so to speak, because the doctor had been alerted by the local police that if anyone showed up with a serious cut from a sharp object, they wanted to know about it. So unbeknownst to me, after we left the hospital, we were reported to the police by the doctor, who knew that we were staying at the DEKE house in Amherst, which is where we headed to from the medical facility. The police arrived at our doorstep shortly after we got there. So we found ourselves in the Northampton County Jail for the remainder of the evening. We were cited for breaking and entering with intent to commit burglary.

The way the law reads you have to have an intent in order to be charged with a felony. Otherwise the charge is just a misdemeanor.

They were trying to stick us with a bigger charge, but we didn't have an intent for burglary—we had an intent for sleep. We were convicted for disturbing the peace.

The next day when I got bailed out and was released from jail, I went over to see my friend's girlfriend to get money to bail him out of jail. I told her that I might be in serious difficulty at Dartmouth because I had had this history of problems up there, and they would probably ask me to leave when they heard about this further problem, but I hoped they wouldn't find out. And she said, "Small chance of that, it's all over the news." And I said, "What are you talking about?" She said that the house we had been accused of breaking into was the national shrine for Emily Dickinson, poet laureate of the country.

So there we were. She gave me the money, I bailed my friend out, and he and I returned to Dartmouth. In those days there was a process for people like me that involved a student body holding a mock trial and then making a recommendation to the authorities of the college, who would then weigh the recommendation and make their own determination and mete out the punishment. The bottom line was we were able to convince the student group that our misbehavior at the Emily Dickinson house was a legitimate mistake due to the late time of the evening and the fact that it was very dark and there were no lights and that the house looked very similar to the DEKE house in all respects. They recommended that we be put on probation with a stern warning but be allowed to complete our studies there.

Amazingly, I was not thrown out of school that year. I squeezed myself through, but I was told it would be very wise for me not to return in my senior year because I probably couldn't stay out of trouble, and since that was the case I probably would not graduate. I persevered, however. I didn't take the advice.

But the real message is that throughout my life I've had to explain that experience. At every job interview they asked about my breaking into the Emily Dickinson house. Once I passed the bar in New York, I had to pass a fitness exam and explain the arrest then. When I became a partner at Lazard Freres, I had to explain to the senior partner what it was all about. It was a lot of baggage to carry through the years. I was always worried that it was going to trip me up—that it would be argued I was unfit because I'd had this experience.

I went back to Dartmouth my senior year and did graduate and went on to law school at the University of Minnesota. I'm amused when I think back on my law school experience that one of the professors, Arthur Miller—who is now a professor of law at Harvard, a brilliant man who was the faculty adviser for the law review when I was an editor on the law review—stopped me one day in the library and said he was puzzled by my college background, because I was a C-minus student yet here I was on the law review and doing honors work. He couldn't understand the discrepancy.

And of course I never said to him that I'd been drunk for four years at college and never opened a book and never went to a class, but it showed the impact the disease had on my ability to manage opportunities that were presented to me, such as an education at a very fine school.

At law school I drank moderately if at all. The bottom line was I loved the subject matter. It just overtook me and I was naturally good at it. I seemed to have that kind of logical mind where the course material was easy for me but very interesting. I graduated cum laude and as a result was hired by the largest law firm in the country at the time, a firm named Shearman & Sterling, on Wall Street.

I graduated from law school in June of 1964 and immediately went to New York. I had no money, particularly as I had married prior to going to law school, so I needed to commence work immediately and was the first of twenty-two new associates to appear for work. I started as a corporate lawyer on Wall Street, where I spent six years. For six years my drinking seemed to be under a little better control, so I was able to maintain an excellent record at the law firm.

However, that period of control soon ended, when I got divorced. My marriage had fallen apart. Shirley and I had two daughters, and after seventeen years together we finally got a divorce; it was completed a few years after I left the law firm. When I quit that firm it was to take a job with a banking client named Lazard Freres. Within two years they made me a partner in the firm, and I went on to have a very successful career as an investment banker on Wall Street. I made more money than I could have possibly imagined. I never considered I would make that much money in my life. I was never focused on becoming a very rich man; that was never an objective of mine. But it turned out to be an ancillary benefit of my experience as a lawyer and as a banker. I built up a substantial net worth of twenty million dollars along the way.

But my alcoholism just got worse. I maintained homes on the East Coast and the West Coast. Two on the East Coast (an apartment in New York and a converted chapel in New Canaan) and two on the West Coast (a townhouse on the beach in Santa Monica and a home in the desert, in Palm Springs, on a golf course out there, since I love to play golf). And at that time I belonged to four different country clubs: Palm Springs, Los Angeles, Manhasset on Long Island, and one in Darien, Connecticut. So I played a great deal of golf, and I was bi-coastal and had all the money I could possibly spend. And as I said, I had divorced earlier from the mother of my two daughters, and then I got remarried to a lady, a lawyer from Los Angeles, who was fourteen years younger than I.

It was a high life in all senses or interpretations of the word. Each Thanksgiving I would invite a group of forty friends to Palm Springs and pay for everything. And my cars! I had a top-of-the-line customized 560 SEC Mercedes convertible that cost $75,000. My wife and I agreed we'd have the top cut off and put on a soft top. That was $25,000 more. She drove her Mercedes SL, which I had painted pink because that was her favorite color, around Beverly Hills. Unbelievable! I seemed to have the world by the throat. I was very comfortable, but my disease got worse yet, and having all the money I could spend didn't exactly help it, because I wound up with an enormous amount of alcohol and wines in all my homes. I'd drink by myself every evening. Eventually, my younger wife got tired of that and decided to divorce me. When that happened my life spun totally out of control.

During that period I was introduced to drugs—something I used to claim I never touched. I wanted nothing to do with drugs and would say silently that I was grateful that when I was in school they didn't have a lot of drugs around. (If they did I was completely unaware of it.) I kind of knew instinctively that I would have succumbed to them in those days. However, in my mind I was above them at this point in my life. But divorce took me right down to where I met a young lady who introduced me to crack cocaine, and I instantly became a crack addict. And naturally because I was interested in the cocaine I wasn't drinking so frequently anymore. My mind told me because I wasn't interested in alcohol I wasn't an alcoholic; this is part of the denial system that most alcoholics suffer from.

I was fifty-seven years old when I got into drugs. I remember later when I got sober going to a doctor at the VA hospital and he turned to me and said, "Do you smoke?" And I said, "No, no I don't smoke." And I said, "Well, maybe an occasional cigar." "No, no," he said, "you smoke." And then I said, "Oh, yes, I did smoke some cocaine." And when I told him about it he said, "Very unusual for a man of fifty-seven to start to smoke crack."

I had just found a different drug that was more compatible with the lifestyle. But the cocaine took me down rapidly.

I was going through a second divorce and was a crack addict and completely irresponsible and out of control! An example was the Mercedes. I had taken it from California and shipped it to New York City. I kept it across the street from my apartment, paying $450 a month for a parking spot. Then one day shortly after it arrived I got a bright idea. Why not just loan it to my drug dealer? He could pick me up in the morning and drive me down to Wall Street to my job. And if I needed some drugs in the morning, he could bring them. Then he could pick me up and take me home, and I'd let him use the car the rest of the day and evening. I'm saving $450 a month!

After two weeks he stopped coming to pick me up. I reported it to the police and to my insurance company, Chubb, a prestigious insurance company, and the guy they sent over asked me the name of the driver. I told him that I only knew his first name, Julio. "You took a $100,000 vehicle and gave it to someone and you don't know his name! Where does he live?" I said, "In Harlem somewhere." Two weeks later I got the divorce decree and didn't own the car anymore and didn't have to worry about where he lived.

Much of my life had been excess. When I was getting the divorce, I took an interest in the value of things and visited a store on Rodeo Drive where my wife had purchased some of the fixtures for the Santa Monica house, and I happened to price the doorknobs that were on the front door of our beach house. They were round bars about two feet long, positioned on each side of the door. You'd push on them and the door would open. They were Lalique crystal and they cost $25,000. That's just a start! I had given my wife carte blanche to do the house however she wanted it. I was out of control, and she was, in my view, too.

At one point in our life we threw a big party at my country club in Darien. Right before we sent out the invitations, the stock market crashed. I can remember that when the date came I addressed all the guests and mentioned that our timing couldn't have been worse. On the other hand, I pointed out that when I looked at the invitations I realized we'd spent so much money on them we couldn't just throw them away . . . those invitations were elaborate!

In the course of this divorce from my second wife, I had three or four different lawyers, and none was satisfactory to me. I was impossible as a client—I was a drug addict. And I wound up losing everything I had. My ex-wife took everything. The court awarded her all of my assets, and I was awarded the liabilities. I wound up with three million in debt and not an asset to my name. It happened because I fired all my lawyers during the divorce period and was unable to show up when the court in California held the hearings for the terms of the divorce.

This was 1994. I was now head of my own small brokerage firm in New York, and for a year I'd been using cocaine. Late that year my family did an intervention. It's a very delicate process to intervene an alcoholic. First of all, alcoholics resent the interference in their lives, and more particularly, they aren't prepared to admit they're alcoholics. So you tell them they are alcoholics and have to go to rehab, and they just bristle if they have any independence at all, and most alcoholics are very independent. So the intervention went very badly. It was done in my office with my brokers present, and they told my brokers what they were doing. I lost total control of my business right there. I couldn't run it anymore; I just had to bail out. No one wanted to work for me after that. I sold the business for a song. My family was right to have an intervention, but the way they went about it was terrible.

After that intervention I thought, "Gee, if my family feels this strongly about it, maybe I should go to rehab." They arranged for me to go to Minnesota to Hazelden. It was supposed to be the Cadillac of the rehab business, so I agreed. They couldn't help me—or rather, I wouldn't let them. It was funny. I sat around a room with a bunch of men, all in recovery purportedly, and everybody had to introduce themselves and acknowledge they were an alcoholic or drug addict—"Hi, I'm Paul, I'm an addict" or "Hi, I'm Paul, I'm a drunk"—in a circle. I would say, "I'm Peter, and I'm from Manhattan." Ha! That sure is all but not admitting you have a problem!

I wasn't ready for that place. I lasted four days and I bailed. I had no money, since my family put me in with no money, and I couldn't get anybody to lend me any because my family had called all my friends and told them not to do anything if I asked. So they had really pissed in the stew, if you will. But I found a friend down in Atlanta, Georgia, that they hadn't contacted and didn't know about, and he wired me money to get an airplane ticket back to New York.

I was living in my apartment in Manhattan as a drug addict with not a nickel to my name as the divorce was proceeding in Santa Monica, California. Under California law they're supposed to split the estate fifty-fifty, and of course the judge found a new way to do that—she gave my wife the asset side and me the liability side of the balance sheet. Primarily because I had no lawyer, I wasn't there myself, and the judge had never liked me. (The reason for that is pretty obvious—I was strung out on something when I was in court.) She just gave my wife everything she wanted and gave me nothing. I had to accept that and it was difficult. I thought on appeal I would win, but I did not because the court said I had thumbed my nose at the lower court and had not shown up for hearings in the process and they weren't going to give me any relief. I had to come to grips with it.

That's what happened to me. And it was the crack addiction that took me down to the point where I was evicted by the sheriff from my apartment because I hadn't paid rent in nine months. I was thrown out on the streets of New York. A homeless person. And of course, I had no contact with my family. They all knew that I was an addict at this point, and no one wanted anything to do with me, which is understandable. So there I was—a former wheeler and dealer who was a multimillionaire reduced to living on the streets of New York.

I had a friend who was a dealer who found me an apartment to share with another addict in Queens at 180th Street and Queens Boulevard. So after a couple of days on the street I found my way up to that apartment and was allowed to sleep on the couch in the living room. Within three or four weeks the person whose apartment that was left. I never saw her again, and eventually I was thrown out of there. But while I stayed at the place in Queens it had no heat, electricity, or hot water. That's how I lived with my disease and my difficult lifestyle. And the bottom hit one day after I awakened in the lobby of the Marriott Hotel on Lexington Avenue. I had crashed there the night before under a table. I got out from under the table and looked around the lobby and saw everyone was very well dressed and realized, "It's Sunday morning." Eventually, I figured out it was Easter Sunday. And I had a moment of clarity. As I walked out of that hotel to go up to the subway two blocks north, I said to myself, "I've got a problem. I had better deal with it."

So I went down in the subway and jumped the turnstile because I had no money and took the train out to 178th Street in Queens. When I got off I found the Yellow Pages and called a rehab and made an appointment to appear as soon as I could, which was two days after that. They said they would send a car and drive me out there, and so I found myself two days later in a car on my way out to Westhampton. I was in rehab for four weeks out there. Didn't have a clue about my disease when I went there, insisted I wasn't an alcoholic during my four weeks, recognized that I was a drug addict, and thought that once I got over the drugs I'd go back to drinking all my wine and alcohol. Going back to drinking was what I was looking forward to.

They disabused me of that thought by pointing out that if nothing else, alcohol would be a gateway for me to go back to my cocaine use. That made a little sense to me. I could understand that. I wasn't happy to hear it, but I realized I was not going to be able to take any of these substances anymore. I was OK. I could live with that; I felt I was strong enough. And when I got out of the rehab after the four weeks, I took a train to New York City and met a nephew of mine who was then matriculating at NYU Law School and had lunch with him. Then he put me on a bus to Newark Airport, whence I flew to Los Angeles on an electronic one-way plane ticket my daughter had sent me.

In Los Angeles my daughter and her husband let me stay at their apartment in Studio City. They had a two-bedroom apartment, so there I was, a recovering drug addict and alcoholic, living at my daughter's house because I couldn't afford an apartment; I had no money and no recourse to money. I spent a month there and was so uncomfortable to be a houseguest in my daughter's home that I insisted I had to get my own apartment; I found one with my daughter's help. My daughter must have put up the security deposit and paid the rent. Anyway, within six months I had a relapse. That began my final fall. I relapsed for thirteen months, and the excuse for relapsing was that I was waiting for my appeal on my divorce, which I was overconfident that I would win. I found a lawyer who was willing to appeal my decision on speculation—I didn't have to pay him anything, and so I didn't have to do anything. I was just waiting to access all my money when the appellate court reversed that decision.

So that court case served as my excuse for not pursuing a sober life. I just went right back out and got hung up with the drugs again, found myself involved with several lower companions, and was very comfortable with them. This was my lowest point. In early 1997 I moved into the home of a drug dealer in Northridge, California, with his porno-queen girlfriend, a couple of "home-boys," and another addict. And within a few months the decision came down on the appeal, and as I said, it did not grant my request to overturn the lower court. So there I was, dead in the water. I had to accept the results. So then I became willing to deal with my addiction. I contacted an old friend of mine who'd been a business associate. It was sort of an accident the way I contacted him. I had agreed to drive a female addict home to her family in Alabama, because she wanted to get out of the rat race that she had buried herself in, just as I had. She had a lot of furniture and needed a Hertz rental truck. I said that when she had it loaded, if she could not find any other driver, I would take her.

Well, I was sitting in my disease one night and there was a knock at the door—I was living with a drug dealer at the time— and there was this young lady. She had the truck outside, and it was time to leave to drive her to Alabama. That night! The one thing I had maintained was my self-image of being responsible. All these drug addicts were not responsible, but I was. That was my pitch. So I was faced with reality. Was I going to welsh on my commitment to her, or was I going to drive her? So I drove her. And I told her I had not a dime in my pocket, and she said she had the money to buy the gas for the truck, and I said OK.

So when we got to Blythe, Arizona, which is a little mobile home community just over the California state line, we decided to crash and sleep for the day, to dry out. When I finally woke up, I checked the truck and saw we needed gas. I told her, and she said she was sorry but she had spent her last dollars on crack just before we left. So she had no money. I was furious. She asked me to call someone to see if I could borrow the money for gas to get her from Arizona to Alabama.

I made a call to an old friend of mine, who agreed to wire us the funds, and he did, and I got her down to Mobile. It took two and a half days. I was detoxing the whole way, and she slept the whole way. I remember driving into her hometown at seven in the morning and I had to wake her up. I told her we had arrived in her town and asked where I was to take her. She said, "Well, what time is it?" I told her it was seven o'clock. And she said, "No one will be home right now. Why don't we get a motel room and spend the day sleeping? Then you can take me home in the evening." Then I said, "I have a better idea." I was scared to death to be observed going into a hotel room in Alabama with a black woman. And so I said, "You drive. You can drop me off at the airport and I'll go ahead to L.A." I got a free ticket by cashing in my frequent flyer miles!

So we went to the airport and she dropped me off, and that was the last I ever heard from her. I was able to get a free ticket into L.A. with my Delta mileage. I called my drug dealer and asked him to meet me when I got into LA, which he agreed to do. He had a car, and he picked me up and took me home and replenished my drug supply on spec. It was shortly after that when I had to call my friend to make arrangements to repay him, and when I did that he said that his boss wanted to see me and could I have lunch with him the following week. I said yes but he'd have to send a car for me, as I had no way to get there.

So they did, and I had lunch, and during lunch his boss offered me a consulting job with a fee of ten thousand dollars. It was a simple project for me, utilizing my legal background more than anything else. I did the job in a couple of days, completed it, got paid, and within a week the ten thousand was all gone on drugs. So I went back for another project. Realizing that I still had problems with my addiction, he arranged to put me in a rehab in Marina del Rey.

It was my third rehab, and the fact is I was ready and it worked. I was there three weeks, and then I was moved to a sober living home in Pasadena, California. My friend paid for all this treatment, and gave me a full-time job consulting, more or less, for the firm, and slowly I got sober in that sober living home. I arrived at the home with all my possessions in my matching luggage from Ralph's grocery store, and I told them I could stay for maybe thirty days. I arrived the first of December 1997, and I said that I was willing to stay until New Year's Day. And I was told that their minimum program was six weeks. "Don't worry," I said. "I'm smart. I'll get it in four." That was the arrogance—the prerecovery attitude. And I wound up staying there seven months because within four weeks I realized I really needed that life, the sober living life, and that facility as an anchor in my sobriety. It took me four weeks to figure it out but I did, and after seven months I was ready to move out and I got an apartment one block away from that house. For more than six years, I used to go to that house every day and sit on the front porch and talk to other recovering alcoholics and drug addicts who were residents of the house at that time. Eventually, I lived farther away, but the bottom line is that's how I got sober.

When I was in the Pasadena sober living house, I started going to a morning AA meeting at 6:15 A.M. right down the street. I would walk to it with a couple of members. I didn't know anything about prayer—never had prayed to a higher power for anything in my life. I was very cynical, and I realized from my brief exposure to recovery that I had to start praying and find a higher power, though I certainly wasn't about to get on my knees. So what I would do on those mornings on the walk to the meeting is I would pray. Walk to the meeting, pray in silence, and then get to the meeting and spend the hour and return to the house. It seemed as though I had my focus, my compass was set, for the day. I knew where I was going and who was guiding me. And I did that for six months. All the time I lived in Pasadena, which was more than six years, I stayed with that recovery meeting. I have recently returned to Pasadena and am living in that sober living home!

During that period I held several different jobs. I tried to get back involved in my area of finance. I had a consulting job with my friend for six months, and then he had to let me go, as he lost control over his company over the ensuing months. After that arrangement I couldn't get work. No one wanted to hire me and no one was interested in interviewing me. I tried to go back to my old firm of Lazard. The senior partner's nose was a mile out of joint because I'd quit on him. And he said, "We don't hire people who quit." And that was that. So I couldn't get back there, and I was told by others who are friends of mine on Wall Street that I shouldn't go back there at all, that it was not a healthy place for me, so I never looked back there again. I did look in the greater Los Angeles area, but I couldn't come up with anything, and it just got very frustrating.

I ended up taking several part-time jobs. I became a courier delivering packages around Hollywood. I had some interesting experiences there. For example, one day I was asked to deliver a package to 1000 Avenue of the Stars, which was a building where I'd had an office on the third floor for many years. And this package had to be delivered to the third floor. When I drove up to that building, I was concerned, in my little messenger outfit, that someone might recognize me because when I had my office I'd get to meet a lot of the tenants and the landlord who was managing the building. Well, I delivered the package, and I had to think as I went up the elevator that God had a sense of humor. He was sending me right back to where I had been and rubbing my nose into it. And it was good for me; it was humbling. Humility was a scarce commodity in my life. So I welcomed it and could see the value.

I delivered these packages for a few months, but it became impossible. I had to pay for my own gas, and I had a car and was struggling to make my car payments, and I had applied for early social security, which I got, and that was what I was living on. Plus I had rent to pay and so forth. I had to work, but this job didn't pay much and I was driving all over hell and back. Every day was a new adventure! One time I had to go down to Anaheim late in the day on a Friday with all the traffic. What a pain in the neck! I couldn't deal with it, so I had to let it go.

At another point I had a job cleaning bathrooms—toilets, sinks, and tubs—to earn a few dollars. Then I got a job making cold calls on the telephone, raising funds for charity, telemarketing. I got fed up with that because I drove sixty miles each way to the office, which was consuming my income.

Then I became a salesman for Sears, selling kitchen cabinet refacing, making cold calls in the greater Los Angeles area. I found myself driving all over the place for that job. It was really discouraging. You had to get a signed contract on the first visit because you never had a second one. My first month I signed a lot of deals and had expectations of getting a reasonably decent salary or commission. But I found out that after I left, within a few days, these people would call and cancel. They weren't supposed to be able to cancel, but Sears was letting them. I realized I was paying the expenses to go to these places, that the company wasn't reimbursing me for my cab or lunch, so it was all on me, and I had no control over the ultimate sale. I'd make the sale and then the company would let them off the hook, apparently for the purpose of promotion. So ultimately I called that quits as well. I was having a very difficult time.

Eventually, I was contacted by a reporter for the *New York Times*, who had heard about my situation at a dinner party and tracked me down through one of my old associates. After the *Times* reported my story in August 2003, I accepted invitations to appear on the "Today" show and "Oprah." This publicity brought me back into the business world where a very good friend called me and hired me as a consultant. He paid me a very good wage. I worked for him for two years, until we terminated the project, and that got me to the point where I was able to move up to Rochester, New York, to live near my sister and her family.

I had a little trouble at the beginning keeping my concentration on projects. My addiction did weaken that ability. But I've always had the ability in terms of the corporate world of doing everything. Because of my legal training I could handle negotiations. I had bank experience and was able to do the opinions that might be required for certain investment banking transactions. And I can do the math work necessary to render opinions. I was blessed. I was full service in my corporate positions because I did it all. Others have observed that I was impatient about being recognized for what I did and showed untimely arrogance. Although it was the drugs that led to my decline, those tendencies were already there and had just been worsened by the chemicals.

Right now I'm struggling again. That was just a two-year deal, which ended a year ago. Since then I've been up here in Rochester trying to make ends meet. I have only social security, which is not enough to live on. I tried consulting and got a project, but that's it, one project.

I've learned that I can adapt. I've learned that it's not all about me. I've learned that money wasn't the solution and though I need to have the benefit of an income, it doesn't have to be in the multiple thousands monthly. I took a job in Rochester working for five weeks removing asbestos from a factory at Kodak Park. I had to quit because my knees swelled up and I have bursitis so it became painful to climb stairs. I couldn't do the job anymore, but it's important to me that, at age seventy, I tried and liked it. I've also learned to let go of resentments. I harbored a resentment against a partner at my law firm. When I got sober I made a list of all my resentments and forgave people—making amends where appropriate but otherwise forgiving people for how I felt they had hurt me. When I did that this particular name went on that list. I had a huge resentment against him. I had to make that resentment list three times, and the third time I realized he was still on the list. But in fact I had evened the score when the client he said I had failed, hired me.

My outlook is transformed. I have a tremendous level of serenity. I'm comfortable in my own skin. Prior to recovery that was never the case. So recovery has given me that. I have two daughters and four grandsons who are active in my life. I have recently moved back to California. My older daughter's husband arranged an electronic ticket to fly me out to see the family. I spent five days with them, which was nice, although I couldn't have paid for the trip. And although I like to keep working and involved in the world, I can accept that and be thankful I'm wanted by children I cherish. My life has had dramatic ups and downs. I went from being a leading lawyer on Wall Street and multimillionaire wheeler-dealer investment banker to a homeless vagrant who was uncontrollably addicted to mind-altering substances. It's a story that could frighten somebody, which makes me laugh, because I am overwhelmed by my present good fortune. There is not a moment I doubt that I have found peace.

*All of those who witnessed my rapid decline*
*Could never have imagined I'd retain my mind*
*All must have expected I'd never return*
*For very few do as we all have learned.*

*But none of these souls could measure my heart*
*Nor could they perceive God's will from the start*
*It is not for man to judge one's fall*
*But better to pray that the fall's not all.*

*Better to extend a hand with a smile*
*And pray again that it's not the last mile*

—"NEVER GIVE UP" BY PETER JAQUITH

# 9

# Michael Glasser

*Today, take away your spell for me.*
*Away from me you have taken it.*
*Far off from me it is taken.*
*Far off you have done it.*
*Happily I recover.*
*Happily my interior becomes cool.*
*Happily my eyes regain their power.*
*Happily my head becomes cool.*
*Happily my limbs regain their power.*
*Happily I hear again.*
*Happily for me the spell is taken off.*
*Happily I walk.*

—PRAYER OF FIRST DANCERS, FROM THE NIGHT CHANT
(NAVAJO HEALING CEREMONY)

Michael Glasser and I ran in similar circles during the halcyon years of the early seventies, when drugs, women, and the pursuit of high times dominated our lives. He was a fast-living big shot from the world of fashion. I was trying to make my mark in show business.

Our paths would cross occasionally at parties and nightclubs or in the home of a hip drug dealer. I only recall glimpses of Michael.

As memory serves, he was a very good-looking guy and was always in the company of beautiful women, which, of course, made me envious—not that I ran with dogs, but I always felt uncomfortable around guys I perceived as having it. And Michael was undoubtedly one of those.

As fate would have it, our love affairs with drugs and the fast life came to a crashing halt at roughly the same time, though I had no idea he was circling the same drain I was. Shortly after I hit my bottom I encountered Michael during one of my very first twelve-step recovery meetings. Wouldn't you know it, I walked into a meeting one night and there he was, sitting next to an absolutely gorgeous woman, who seemed to be joined to his hip. I greeted him with a shade of embarrassment over the events in my life that led me to this place, but I realized that Michael must have also hit some major bumps in his road.

People in early recovery are like passengers who survived a train wreck. Gratitude and camaraderie prevail. Michael and I became sober buddies and spent much time together at meetings, on the phone, and in general support of the new path our lives had taken.

Not long after we became friends in the program I started to hear about trouble Michael was in with the law. I learned that he had been arrested for some big drug dealings, and I thought to myself, "Aha, so that's why he's doing the recovery thing. He's hoping to get the heat off of himself by coming into the program. Still the scammer I thought he was."

But as time passed and I kept seeing Michael at meetings and talking with him more and more often on the phone, I came to believe that he was for real in his desire to stop using and make an honest effort at getting and staying clean. I also got to know his girlfriend Veronica, who I thought was as sincere in her pursuit of sobriety as anyone I knew at the time. She was a great influence on Michael, and I grew to admire her tremendously.

During our first year of recovery I witnessed Michael go through an experience with the law and facing up to the crime he allegedly committed that deeply impacted the way I felt about him and the way I was coming to feel about recovery in general. But let Michael tell you this story in his own words. . . .

---

## MICHAEL GLASSER

The very first time I had a drink I went into a blackout and threw up. And the very last drink I had I went into a blackout and threw up. So it never really changed for me. The shocking part of my story is that for twenty-seven years, I was the only one who didn't know I had a problem. I don't think I'm a dumb person, I think I know what's going on around me, yet for many, many years I denied my reality.

My first drink was when I was thirteen, at a wedding. My mother, who was an alcoholic, got drunk and undressed at the wedding, and I was really embarrassed. I remember sitting there, having a couple of drinks to hide my embarrassment, and then passing out. I remember being appalled at seeing my own mother doing something like that. Years later, when I was drinking and using drugs, I would go into a blackout in any restaurant you want to name in L.A. and I'd get undressed. I'd wake up the next morning and I could never figure out what compelled me to take off my clothes in public. But when I was in the hospital in treatment, they made me write about my drinking and using, and I realized the connection to my mother.

I was astonished. I would go to any length to please my mom, even in a blackout. She took off her clothes, and I thought it was disgusting, but I did it also. That's just one of the many things I've learned about myself in sobriety. My actions and where they all come from.

I was an athlete when I was young, so I didn't drink much or use drugs at all. I was the only one in my crowd that didn't do drugs. I was playing basketball, and this or that sport, and I prided myself on my health. After graduating high school, I didn't go to college because my brother had screwed up in school, so I went to work in the clothing industry. I started going out with models, but I was still very controlling in the way I lived. I only drank occasionally, and I never thought I had a problem. But as we know, alcoholism is a progressive disease.

At the beginning of my career in the industry, I was a designer and a salesman. I would start something and would always screw it up. Everyone would say to me, "You're such a genius, Michael." And I would look at them and think, "Yeah, I'm such a genius, but I'm a loser." I started to use with ever-increasing frequency—primarily cocaine—and my work would occasionally suffer accordingly. I never did connect my behavior with what was going on in my business. The bottom line was if you gave me plastic and told me it would get me high, I would eat the plastic. After a while, it really made no difference what substance I used, I just needed to get out of it. I didn't like myself, and I had no confidence in my social abilities. I did have confidence in my athletic ability, in work or with a bunch of guys, but once you threw the element of women into the situation, I had no confidence.

So I started using more and more drugs. I was young and making a lot of money. I started this fashion business, which became a big success. A guy I knew asked me if I wanted to move out to California. That was 1971. That's when everything started happening for me. The California lifestyle, the drugs, and I had this great business relationship. Then came all the girls. My whole life became wrapped around making enough money so I could give it to my drug dealer, so I could get my drugs on Friday night and party all weekend.

Needless to say, my business would eventually go down the tubes. But I didn't know that then. I knew I was having a ton of fun, and for many years I did have a lot of fun. Toward the end of my drinking and using, I got involved in a scheme. I feel so stupid each time I tell this story, that I actually didn't realize what was going on. I thought it was something legitimate.

A woman calls me up and wants to come to California and put money in the bank—$10,000 or more—but they don't want the banks to report it. If I could arrange that I would get 17 percent of everything they deposited.

As ridiculous as it sounds, I agreed to do it. You have to understand, at this time my businesses were not doing very well. I wasn't a big-shot fashion designer anymore, and this seemed like a way for me to start making some serious money again. I had no connections at banks, so I would just go from one to another, stupidly asking if they would do this. One of the banks I approached went to the government and told them there was a guy who came in trying to set up a money-laundering account. So they set up a sting.

The first deposit I made into this bank/sting was $100,000. A week later this same woman calls me and says, "Listen, I have a couple kilos of cocaine. Do you think you could sell it?" How this woman ever found me in the first place, I still don't know. I said, "No, I've never done that, but I could give it a shot. I certainly know enough people who buy drugs."

So she brings me two kilos of coke and I probably sold it in forty-five minutes. I called her and said, "It's gone," and she said, "Great, we have another ten kilos coming here." So, soon, I had this whole drug-dealing operation, and a money-laundering operation, and I'm doing more drugs than ever. I now weigh 150 pounds and I'm off the wall. Consequently, I got fired from the operation. The shortfall was too great. I was spending lots of money and using the drugs. I went through a kilo myself. I even flushed drugs down the toilet by mistake once. There was all kinds of stupid stuff happening.

Now we get to the time just before I got sober. I had totally lost control of myself. I weighed 220 pounds from drinking and eating nothing but junk. I hadn't bathed, shaved, or brushed my teeth in about six weeks. I was living in a friend's apartment in North Hollywood, and the only thing I wanted to do was kill myself. That's what I really wanted to do. I was totally disgusted with myself. I had a few dollars in my pocket, four or five dollars usually, and I'd go to the liquor store and buy a quart bottle of Popov vodka. I'd come back to my friend's place and take the empty bottle of Stolichnaya that was in the freezer and pour the Popov into the Stoli bottle. I wanted people to know, if they came over to this place, that I was still flush. Now, understand that no one ever came over, but I'd do this routine every day.

I used to tell my friend Norman that one day I would have the balls to blow my brains out. I'd tell him, "I can't live this way." So Norman would always call me. Once or twice a day, just to see if I'd pick up the phone, and if I did, everything was cool.

One day Norman got a whole bag of bootleg quaaludes. The next day he called, and I didn't answer the phone. I had taken twenty-odd quaaludes and my Popov vodka, and I was out on the floor. When I didn't answer the phone, he called 911, and the EMS arrived, knocked down the door, and found me dead.

They shocked me three times and brought me back to life and took me to Riverside Hospital. I remember being in a tunnel and hearing a voice. And the voice was telling me "You'll be OK," to which I responded "No." I really don't know what to make of this moment, but I do remember it and think about it every day. I remember waking up, and the first conscious thought I had was, "Michael, there is something terribly wrong, but you need help."

That was the very first time in my life that I didn't blame anybody but myself and that I actually admitted that I needed help.

That day my dad was flying out to California to celebrate his eighty-fifth birthday. That was my present to him—for him to find me in the emergency room in Riverside Hospital. When I left there I immediately went into a rehab at South Bay Hospital. I was there for twenty-seven days and took to what was going on there. I knew I had a problem with drugs, but I never thought I had a problem with alcohol, until I started to delve into my creepiness.

When I was twenty-seven days sober, I got out of the hospital and was living on my brother's couch in Santa Monica. One day there was a knock on the door, and it was the DEA, who had come to arrest me for my role in the drug-dealing/money-laundering sting. I tried to explain to them that I was fired from that deal, but they refused to listen to me. Here's something ironic: one of the guys from the DEA who came to arrest me was in recovery. It's nothing big, but he told the other agents not to handcuff me. It might be insignificant to other people, but to me it was a message.

I was taken to the prison on Terminal Island. I remember I was allowed one phone call. There was no bail. They arrested twenty-five of us the same day. It was a real big case, a very high-profile case. It was in all the newspapers. So I called my dad, and he told me he could get me out as long as I didn't have any outstanding warrants. I don't know about anyone else, but my m.o. was not to pay traffic tickets, and I was absolutely sure I had warrants. So what happened that day was a miracle:

It was the beginning of a long July Fourth weekend, which meant I would be incarcerated three days before I could see a judge. But the jailer came to my cell and said I could go. The computers were down so they couldn't check to see if I had any warrants, so they just let me go. Maybe that is another insignificant event, but to me it was another message. From that moment on, for the first time in my life, I did things I was supposed to do. I joined a twelve-step recovery program and got a sponsor. I made all new friends in that program. I showed up and went to meetings every day. I wasn't working because I couldn't get a job. I was a high-profile guy in a very negative way.

I'd go to two or three recovery meetings a day, and this one guy would say to me, "Come on, Michael, let's go run." He said we would run until the negative thoughts left my head—"And when they do, we'll stop." And we did this every day. The guy was a very slow runner, and it drove me crazy, but that's what we did. We'd run ten miles, then twelve miles, fifteen miles, sixteen miles, and some of the voices would stop. The voices were telling me, "You're going to prison." This guy kept telling me, "You just go on with your life" and "You should get a job." But I wondered, "How can I get a job? Who's going to hire me?"

I don't know how it happened, but some company in Roanoke, Virginia, that had no idea what was happening in Los Angeles, California, hired me to be a consultant in the clothing industry. So I started back to work. It wasn't a big deal, but I was working. Though I was also facing being sentenced to prison. My sponsor in the recovery program said to me, "Michael, you have to go to the authorities and confess to them everything you did." I said, "They don't know everything I did. I know the charges against me." I had a court-appointed lawyer, I had no money, and I had a sponsor telling me to confess to everything I did.

I just couldn't do it, I was too afraid. And he said to me one day, "Michael, here's the deal. If you don't do it, you'll probably drink again, and I'm not going to be your sponsor." And that was enough for me to tell my court-appointed lawyer, "I'm going downtown and I'm going to tell them what I did." And he said, "OK, but let me go down there first and make a deal." I said, "Sure, good idea." He came back and said, "No deal." So I said, "Well, I still have to go down there." And he said, "No, you can't." I said, "Yes, I can, with you or without you."

We made the appointment and went down there. The U.S. attorney was named Robert Perry. He's a judge now. We went into his office, and I said, "I came here to confess because my sponsor told me to tell you everything I did. Not what anyone else did, but just what I did."

And I told him the whole story. That I was involved from the beginning. That I was dealing drugs, that I was doing this, that I was doing that. He looked at me and said, "We'll check this out and we'll get back to you."

About a week later, he called me, and so I went back to his office with the court-appointed lawyer. And he said to me, "You know, Michael, no one ever came to us like this before. Your story checked out, but you're still going to prison, no matter what."

I remember walking out of that U.S. attorney's office and calling my sponsor and saying, "Ed, do you realize what you just made me do?" And here's what he said to me: "Michael, God wouldn't take you this far to drop you on your ass." And he hung up the phone. I didn't know what that meant. All I knew was I was floored.

I had such shame about what was going on. What I did do, though, was show up for work. And show up for meetings and do what I was supposed to do. Every once in a while, the U.S. attorney would call me and say, "You know, one of my DEA agents is having a problem—would you mind taking him to a meeting?" There was no conning bullshit thought about it on my part. It was, "Absolutely, absolutely, I'll take him to a meeting." I never wondered if they were checking up on me or manipulating me. Nothing like that. My thoughts and actions were clean and pure. And it happened quite a few times that I took agents to meetings.

Then came the day of reckoning. I remembered what the U.S. attorney had said to me: "Regardless of what the probation department recommends, you're going to prison." There was a voice inside of me. A real quiet, quiet little voice. And that quiet voice said, "Everything is going to be OK."

There was also a loud voice that told me what they were going to do to me, but I listened to the quiet voice.

When it was time for my sentencing, I was living with a girl at the time. I was going to meetings. I had a great group of friends, and life was going on. When I went to the authorities I pled guilty, so the case was over for me. But there were many others charged—it was a big case. The day came and I'll never forget it: August 1, 1983. The hearing was at 1:30 P.M. I know that because there were three recovery meetings going on over on the west side of L.A. At 1:30 those three meetings stopped to say a prayer for me. The court was filled with people from my twelve-step program. I remember my genius court-appointed lawyer said that letters mean shit, but my sponsor said, "Get as many letters as you can," and that's what I did. I had gotten as many letters as I could.

The sentences they were handing out were pretty harsh. I believe ten years was the lightest sentence given to anybody. Then came my name, and I remember the judge saying, "This is the hardest sentence I have to hand out." I couldn't fathom what that meant, but what happened next was amazing. That U.S. attorney that said I was going to prison "no matter what" got up before the judge and literally begged him not to put me in jail.

I was stunned. The reason he gave was that I was trying to change my life *prior* to them catching me. I wasn't trying to change my life just to influence my sentencing. I OD'ed, I died, I was brought back to life, and I got into recovery. It wasn't something I had wanted to do at the time, but for some reason the U.S. attorney was impressed that I was in recovery when they caught me. He used that to appeal to the judge.

The judge then looked down at me and asked if I had anything to say. At that moment I thought about how I never really grasped what I had done. I never really thought it was that big a deal or that it could have hurt that many people, but in that courtroom at that moment I realized now despicable my actions were. I broke down when I realized how bad the things I did really were. It was a cleansing moment.

Then the judge pronounced his sentence. He gave me five years' probation. All of the people who were there to support me stood up, and we formed a circle and said the Lord's Prayer. A counselor of mine from Riverside Hospital, as we were saying the Lord's Prayer, nudged me and said, "Never forget where that verdict came from. The judge said the words, but that was God's verdict."

It was through this experience that I found a God that I never had. I found that if you live a certain way, things can change. What I've learned about my life since I've gotten sober is when I choose to live in the truth, as painful as it might be at any given moment, that I will come out the other side whole. I lived an absolute truth through that experience and came out whole.

I can't tell you that my life has been perfect since then. It's not that way. God gave me a will and I still have to screw with it. During that time I was with this girl. We got married. I was crazy in love with her. We started a business together that was tremendously successful. For whatever reason, I still didn't believe that I should be successful, I didn't have enough faith in my higher power, and I ended up sabotaging my success.

I was an active alcoholic in denial for twenty-seven years of my life. It's the same thing in other areas of my life. I've denied my own truth, until it's too late sometimes. I screwed that business up, mainly because I screwed up the marriage and had stopped going to meetings. I've done some terrible, terrible things in sobriety. I'm not proud of this at all, but the worst things I've done were to the mother of my children. I had an affair while she was pregnant with our second child, and I left her for that woman. And that's when I lost our business. I can never forgive myself for that. The whole time I was with that woman I lived in fear that God was going to punish me.

So, I lost that business after I had been sober for about ten years. I had stopped going to meetings. I hadn't gone for a long time. I didn't go because I was embarrassed. I was embarrassed about my behavior. I was living with a woman who drank a lot, and the miracle is that I never drank. But here's what happens when you live like that. At seventeen years sober I was on a cliff in Malibu, in a car, and I was going to drive off the cliff. I made one phone call, to my ex-wife, the woman that I had so screwed over. And she said to me, "Is that the legacy you want to leave your kids?" And I couldn't do it.

I was a total bust, and she took me in and let me live on her couch for a while. This woman that I so hurt. There's something about people in sobriety that other people don't know. How people reach out to each other and care. My ex-wife Veronica is my best friend. I love her more than any human being alive because she's allowed me to be me, and she's helped me through so much.

From that day on, at seventeen years sober, I started showing up again. I started attending meetings again, and I went to work, consulting for a company called Lucky Jeans. I met a guy and we hit it off; we came up with an idea for another business. We created this business, called Seven Jeans—a business beyond belief. The reason this happened was because of my sobriety. I learned in my sobriety that it's not always about me. I can't do it by myself. I need help. I was able to find somebody to work with when I don't have to be the big shot. We are equals, and we created this amazing business.

My life has so drastically changed. Monetary success is one thing, but my success has too much to do with my children and my ex-wife. The tools that I got in sobriety are amazing.

For example, when you're in the creative end of the business I'm in, you live in fear that your competitors will get there before you. Every time I flew to New York, I had to go to this certain store so I could find the right stuff before any of my competitors found it.

I remember reading this book, *A New Pair of Glasses* by Chuck C., which had a profound effect on me. It's all about finding a new perspective in life. Chuck said that people would sit in this chair at his home looking out the window, which overlooked the Pacific Ocean (he lived in Laguna Beach), and he always asked them what they saw. And he was amazed that everyone saw it differently.

I had just finished this book and I was in New York. A friend of mine, Peter, whom I went to high school with, and who's sober the same amount of time as I am, was going to meet me for lunch. But that meant I couldn't go to the stores first. So I was walking down the street to meet Peter, and I remembered what Chuck said—that everyone sees things differently. And from that moment I realized, "I don't have to rush anymore. What I see I see, what I feel I feel, and it's mine. And everyone out there has their own experience." It calmed me down. I lost that nagging fear that you were going to "beat" me to "it." Whatever "it" was.

What I know today is the gift that I've been given comes so graciously from God. I have no formal education. I didn't go to design school, I can't draw, I can't do anything. But here's what I have—a vision. A vision I get and I clearly see it. All I need is someone to translate what I see. You know how I know I'm finished with a new clothing line? I know I'm finished when I sleep through the night. Then I know the line is finished.

So I've taken all these tools I've acquired in my sobriety and applied them to my life. And I love my life today. In fact, I'm in awe of how much I can love. The fact that I love my children is amazing to me. I came from a place where there was no love. And now love has become my primary purpose.

When I was out there drinking and using, messing up my life, the thing I thought about was, "I'm going to leave my kids nothing." It wasn't what I wanted. I hoped to leave them with something, so they could have an easier time than I did.

I've done what I've done in sobriety by living my life one day at a time. And all of a sudden it's twenty-seven years later, and I look around and say, "Holy Cow, how did I get here from there?" I've gone through so much, but I think the greatest gift is that I actually like myself today. Knowing I'm an imperfect human being trying to get better.

If someone said to me, "Michael, you are going to die tomorrow, let's get loaded," my answer would be, "No. I want to feel the experience." I've gotten so much in these past twenty-seven years. I'm truly a grateful alcoholic.

# 10

# Guerin Swing

*A man doesn't have time.*
*When he loses he seeks, when he finds*
*he forgets, when he forgets he loves, when he loves*
*he begins to forget.*

—YEHUDA AMICHAI, "A MAN IN HIS LIFE"

Guerin Swing grew up in the design business in Los Angeles. He is a third-generation interior designer who has made his living with his artistic designs and installations. After Guerin completed design school, he taught numerous classes and seminars at local universities and colleges in California. He launched his design career in response to being asked to showcase and lend his expertise to many of the interior design model houses.

Since then, Guerin's designs have been seen on or in E! Entertainment Television, "Entertainment Tonight," "MTV Cribs," "The Oprah Winfrey Show," "Geraldo Rivera," "Lifestyles of the Rich and Famous," and the *Enquirer, People, Angeleno, Interior Design, Flaunt,* and *Los Angeles* magazines, as well as many other local shows, newspapers, and periodicals.

In addition to being an artist and designer, Guerin is also a member of the Set Painters Union and a licensed contractor. Because of these factors, he is asked to do historical renovations in and around California, including the world-famous Roosevelt Hotel. He specializes in custom finishes and has been asked by top distribution companies of his mediums to instruct their employees on how to best utilize their products. At Guerin Design and Development, some of the installations he has done include the use of color washes, glazes, sealants, metallic powders, waxes, plasters, cements, metals, paints, and specialty tools.

Most recently, Guerin has completed multiple projects on the Sunset Strip in Hollywood and Rodeo Drive in Beverly Hills: Bulgari, Bally's Clothing, Le Dome, Katana, Chi at the Sunset Hyatt, Clafoutis, and the above-mentioned Roosevelt Hotel. Other projects include the Chrome Hearts Showroom, Mediterraneo Restaurant, the Pig and Whistle, the Sunset Room, Bastide Restaurant, Ivy by the Shore, Radisson Huntley Hotel, Concorde Club, the White Lotus, and Black Steel Restaurant.

A partial list of some of the high-end individual clients Guerin has done projects for include Wayne Brady, Emmy award–winning talk show host; Leeza Gibbons, NBC talk show host; Ryan Seacrest, "American Idol" host; Mark McGrath, TV personality and lead singer for the rock band Sugar Ray; Fred Durst, lead singer for the rock band Limp Bizkit; Jonathon Davis, lead singer for the rock band KORN; Scott Humphrey, music producer; Tommy Lee, rock star; Pamela Anderson, actress; Ashlee Simpson, TV star and musician; Halle Berry, movie star; Wolfgang Puck, world-renowned chef; and Simon Cowell, "American Idol" judge.

## GUERIN SWING

Guerin, which is my first name, is more than just a name for me. At a young age, in around fourth grade, I started feeling out of place because of it. Teachers always pronounced it wrong.

It always made me feel different. I handled it by correcting them every time—"No, my name is Guerin" (pronounced Garrin). And perhaps I was a bit different. I first got in trouble in the fourth grade. I went to a private school where we had to wear a suit and a tie. I got in such trouble at that school! One day I showed my penis to the other kids in the class. This got me thrown out of school. As it happens, I didn't understand that this was wrong. Even though this was a very expensive private school adjacent to Beverly Hills, they still kicked me out for acting up.

I also remember my parents telling me outlandish stories from the tabloids, like, "Man puts baby in oven and tries to cook him." My mother would say, "That's because he's on drugs." Or, "Mother jumps off building and tries to fly," and she'd say "That's because she's on drugs." My mother would relate these outlandish news items on the way home from school. They would impact my mind because they were so scary.

But as scary as my parents tried to make drugs and alcohol sound, they were still very alluring to me. They had a very nice bar in their house, and they would have cocktail parties. These were very glamorous affairs. My parents were interior designers and had a beautiful home like you would see in a magazine. At these parties there would be alcohol, lots of alcohol, and a lot of really nice different shaped glasses. My parents would let me come behind the bar and help out putting ice in the glasses. They taught me, at a very young age, how to make mixed drinks. In effect, I was bartending at a very young age. Even with alcohol being easily accessible, it wasn't something I was really into yet.

In the seventh grade, junior high school, is where my story of abuse really begins. I was a preppy kid, and everybody at my school was into heavy metal—they had long hair and listened to the rock 'n' roll most adults hated. There were gang members and skate-boarders, punk rockers and new-wavers, and I just didn't fit in. I didn't fit in with the rich kids, either; I didn't feel I belonged to that crowd. I just didn't fit in at all, and I longed to fit in so badly. I know this is something that a lot of alcoholics can relate to!

One day a bunch of us were at the liquor store, and someone stole a bottle of vodka and a bottle of orange juice. We made screwdrivers. We drank like a gallon of the stuff. I was feeling pretty wasted. I was probably acting a bit more drunk than I actually was. I'd never ditched school before, and my friends wanted to, so I said, "If I can't walk a straight line, I'll ditch school." So I proceeded to ditch school.

I had gotten drunk for the first time and had ditched school for the first time, and we were hiding behind a house when one of the kids said, "I've got some pot. Does anybody want to smoke marijuana?" I said, "OK," and I tried it. Just then another kid comes running out of the house we were hiding behind and yells, "Run, it's the cops!" The kid was a burglar and had just robbed the house. So here was my day: I got drunk, I ditched school, I smoked pot, and I got chased by the cops, all within a couple of hours. That was the beginning of my journey.

I made it back to school that day, but some of the kids got in trouble. Some even got arrested. But I didn't. What happened to me though was I was accepted. I was "in." I was "that guy." This was something I had never felt before. I was like a hero. After that we would smoke pot every morning at the liquor store and buy Big Gulp containers and fill them with alcohol we had stolen from our parents' houses. I had an Army canteen that I would fill with alcohol and bring to school. We thought we were so smooth walking around the school with our alcoholic drinks. You could also walk into the bathroom at any time and smoke pot. Kids were in there constantly getting high. We even smoked pot in class. I remember a teacher once standing up and saying, "Do I smell marijuana?" And that was the funniest thing I had ever heard. We all laughed and thought, "Yeah, but what the hell are you going to do about it?"

Needless to say, my education went into the can. By seventh grade it had come to a halting stop. I pretty much just drew pictures all day. When I reached the ninth grade, I was taking seventh-grade remedial classes. In the tenth grade, I had a girlfriend—the high school drug dealer, naturally—whose mother sold drugs from her house. I was in the tenth grade and she was a senior. Because I was dating a senior, I was the most popular guy on campus. She was as beautiful as could be, but she was dealing drugs. By that time, I was doing cocaine, hallucinogens, mushrooms, acid, and all the gateway drugs. To me cocaine and mushrooms were nothing, kids' play. But sticking to strictly using didn't last long. Soon I was dealing drugs.

In the eleventh grade, I got kicked out of every class except art class. I sat in the counselor's office from morning until the end of day. I never ditched school anymore, though, because that's where the party was. I went every day. I was finally kicked out of high school and sent to a continuation school, which was the worst thing imaginable. It was a work-at-your-own-pace school. You could smoke cigarettes, and you could come to school with a hangover and sleep in class. That's what I did. Coke and alcohol all night, and I'd come home at all hours. Finally, my parents had had enough and kicked me out of the house.

I was seventeen years old, and I moved to Hollywood. Crack central. I was introduced to crack cocaine, which I initially smoked every couple of days and on weekends, but soon it was all the time. I found a new girlfriend, who introduced me to speed. I ended up moving in with her and started shooting up speed. I was beginning to get pulled over by the police, and since I had a ton of unpaid tickets, I often went to jail. It became routine— getting pulled over by the cops. Of course, I was doing illegal things—dealing drugs, stealing alcohol from liquor stores, and any number of other things—but I kept getting locked up for those unpaid tickets.

One morning someone woke me up and I discovered that my whole apartment had been ransacked at some point during the night. I said, "What happened?" And he said, "I don't know. You trashed your whole apartment and your girlfriend's in the hospital. You punched out her front teeth." I had no recollection of this, and he said, "The police are on the way over, so you better go." I tell this story because that's where drugs and alcohol got me. I'd go into a blackout, wake up, and say, "Tell me what I did."

My life at that time was a big roller coaster. I came from a good family, did lots of drugs, and got in trouble with the police. I would clean up for a couple of days and get right back into it again.

That went on for at least eight years. I would get all kinds of great opportunities to do things in my life, but I would invariably mess them up. I'd get a great job and go out and celebrate and then not come to work the next day. I was completely self-destructive; I never felt worthy. When good things came to me, I screwed them up.

I wanted to be an artist. I thought being an artist meant you were completely smashed on drugs, falling out of a town car in front of a gallery show of your work, proclaiming, "I'm here, I've arrived." That was my dream. So I did my thing and did have many art shows, but none were a success, because I was completely strung out on drugs. I remember being so high on coke I could hardly speak. Obviously, I wasn't selling anything because I couldn't talk. Being high was my primary goal I sought and I did achieve that, but it didn't get me anywhere.

Unbelievably, I was a functioning drug addict and alcoholic. I had a company, and I had employees. I wasn't making much money, but I was surviving. I should also mention that I continued dealing drugs during all this time—nothing big, but enough to pay my rent. Art never really paid my bills.

The end of my using went something like this. I'd wake up in the morning, smoke some pot, eat a bowl of cereal, snort or shoot speed all night long while I was doing my "art," and then at around four in the morning, I'd smoke some heroin to go to sleep. Then I'd wake up in the morning and do it all over again.

I couldn't stop drinking or using drugs. I was miserable knowing that I would wake up each day and have to use. It sucked. My life was completely unimaginable. It was like going to a movie. Two hours of enjoyment followed by twenty-two hours of hell.

There were these two guys who worked for me who would come in at nine every morning and bring a pot of coffee. They were on time every day and they were sober. It seemed bizarre to me. The other people who worked for me were addicts and drunks who would show up between ten and eleven, hung over and wasted from the previous night. So I told these two guys that I was going to clean up for a year. I was doing a job for this guy and I went into his office and said, "I feel like shit, and I picked a bad day to get sober." He said, "What did you just say?" And I said, "I picked a bad day to get sober." And he said, "You picked a great day to get sober." Without knowing it, I was talking to my Eskimo.*

---

*Eskimo story—well known in the rooms of recovery meetings. . . . A man walks into a bar, takes a seat, and orders a drink. Over the next few rounds the customer and bartender get into a heated discussion over the existence of God. The customer, to illustrate his belief that there is no God, tells the bartender how he was recently stranded in the wilds of Alaska, alone, lost, and freezing to death. He began to pray to God, "If you do exist, *please* save me. Don't leave me here in the wilderness." "Well," the bartender says, "that proves it. Here you are alive and well and obviously rescued by this God you didn't believe in." "Naw," says the customer, "some damn Eskimo came along and showed me the way out."

Then he asked me, "Can you stay sober until eight o'clock tonight?" I said, "Yeah, sure I can." And he said, "I want you to meet me at this meeting." I went to the meeting, which was in Hollywood, and I couldn't believe it—I knew at least ten people there. I saw many people I knew from the streets, who I knew had been using, but they weren't out there anymore. They were in the meetings.

I wish I could say from that day forward I stayed sober, but it took me about six months before I really understood the program. I had a hard time, but I did go to meetings. I didn't have time to go to rehab, nor could I afford it—I had to keep working. I went to at least two meetings a day for the first ninety days. I'd go to a noon meeting, go back to work, and then go to one at night. Eventually, I got a sponsor, and then I broke my leg in a snowboarding accident. What he told me was that God was trying to slow me down. I had been going a hundred miles an hour in every direction. I was a hyperactive guy, coming off speed—I had no discipline. I was a newcomer with a broken leg and I was walking with a cane. Everyone was saying, "God wants you to slow down." And they were right: this accident did slow me down so I could stop and smell the flowers.

While I was in the hospital, I told off my first sponsor because he didn't return my call when I phoned him. I left him a nasty message, and he finally called me back and said, "Don't you ever talk to me like that again, and don't you ever call me again." And he hung up on me. That incident made me realize that I better not talk to anyone like that again.

So I went and got a new sponsor; I did the steps, which I didn't do perfectly. I've been sober now over ten years, and I've gone through all of the steps at least three times. All the things I've learned in my twelve-step program I have applied to my business. In sobriety, because of the twelve-step meetings, I've learned how to show up on time. I've learned how to make a commitment—do what I say, say what I mean. I'm an interior designer, designing famous people's homes. I've designed big restaurants and hotels, and I accomplish this all because I'm sober.

I now believe that if you suit up and show up on time and do what you say you're going to do, you'll be a success. Sometimes, it really is that simple. Back when I was using, I could never show up on time. That was a joke: I could never show up at all! I would get great jobs and not show up for them. Today, I don't bullshit and don't lie. People told me that if I made a list of all the things I wanted, I'd be selling myself short. For example, when I first got sober I was thinking "small time"—just enough money for gas for my old 1986 truck and enough to pay the rent. Today I own my own home, I have three Harley Davidson motorcycles, I just bought my wife a new car. I have an office with twenty employees. In it I have my own office where I can close the door! I have things I never dreamed of. People hand me big checks with my name on them, and I don't run to Las Vegas with them. Imagine, I actually deposit a check in the bank. I remember getting a thousand dollars for a job and going to a check-cashing place because I didn't have a bank account, then waiting a couple of hours to get it cashed and going to buy drugs. That was how I lived. I don't live like that anymore.

Today I have serenity. I never understood what that word meant. It may have taken me a little longer than others to find it, but the other day I left my office at about 8 P.M. I had worked late, and all of a sudden I had this feeling of being comfortable in my own skin. I told my wife and she said, "That's called serenity, Guerin." I needed to have it pointed out to me!

In my sobriety I met my wife. She has been sober for twenty-six years, and we have a great relationship. Four years ago she got cancer, and I stood by her side, and my friends in my recovery program helped me walk through this with her. The old me would have never stayed. If you had cancer or were near death, I'd leave because I couldn't deal with it. I would be loaded, that's for sure. But in this situation with my wife, I didn't use or drink, and I'm with her every step of the way. She has been three years in remission. She lost all her hair; she had both her breasts removed. I'm still with her, and I love her so much. We have two beautiful children who have never seen me drink.

Sobriety is the best thing that ever happened to me.

# 11

# Wiktor Osiatynski

*Behold, I do not give lectures or a little*
*Charity*
*When I give I give myself.*

—WALT WHITMAN, SONG OF MYSELF

As we follow Wiktor Osiatynski, international legal scholar and authority on individual rights, from his office in a handsome new building in the middle of the University of Connecticut College, where his class on comparative human rights convenes, to a larger, airier lounge, we think that his presence is proof of UConn's advancement into a major university. An adviser to George Soros and a member of the board of the Open Society Foundation, Wiktor is also a man you call on if your country is writing a national constitution with humanistic and democratic ideals.

Wiktor has also taught at the University of Warsaw, from which he holds degrees in law and sociology, as well as the University of Budapest, Antioch, Stanford, Columbia, the University of Chicago, and Harvard Law School. He has written, in Polish, seventeen books, mostly about political science and also *Rehab*, which is translated to English—a look back twenty years on his early recovery from alcoholism. He has had an impact on treatment of alcoholism in Polish prisons and in Eastern Europe generally. He is a lion of a man—he reminds me of Rod Steiger. His eyes smile constantly, yet he has no palpable gestures, his demeanor and a sort of massive physicality communicate the weight of thought, like a powerful jurist's, and peace.

As Wiktor speaks steadily in a quiet voice, I think of his teaching. I wish I could take his course, and I wonder whether he is a tough grader who motivates students to the limit or an easy grader who creates a peaceful setting for optimal learning. He might prefer, I decided, if the administrations permitted, that students assign their own grades, as calling on one's best behavior is how this man lives.

Ewa Woydyllo, Wiktor's wife, whom he speaks of in this interview, has suggested that someone in recovery is day-to-day walking up an escalator coming down, yet if there is that sense of struggle about Wiktor, there is also joy at being who he is where he is—the intellectual and emotional grist that both his field and his recovery present. He is also fiercely independent and doesn't want to be fenced in. About his credentials he remarked, "Professionally, I don't know my identity."

You could hardly find a person more committed to the recovery movement. Early in sobriety, Wiktor says, he spoke with a woman in Spain and realized he knew 90 percent of who she was from sharing recovery: "To be friends we say in Polish you have to eat a barrel of salt together. With another alcoholic we already ate three-fourths of a barrel of salt."

---

# WIKTOR OSIATYNSKI

I have been an alcoholic probably most of my life. Even before I picked up my first drink, which I hardly remember. I do remember drinking a homemade liquor made from sour cherries with my brother when I was eight. We liked the taste of these cherries, so we drank half a gallon of this alcoholic fermentation of sour cherries, after which I got very sick. Yet I sort of liked it. I liked the taste of it.

My drinking lasted for twenty-one years, between the ages of seventeen and thirty-eight. But even when I became a full-fledged alcoholic, I didn't like the taste of the alcohol, but I did like the taste of sherry and cherry vodka. I now realize that maybe that is related to my first experience.

I remember drinking again when I was in high school and went to some track event. I was sitting next to a soldier who was on leave from his army unit. We became friendly. He was on leave for a few days and wanted some company, so we got a bottle of wine and then another bottle of wine. And I got very drunk and went home and vomited and made a mess. These were the beginnings that I can really remember.

In high school I started hanging around with older boys. I had an older brother and I wanted to be like him. How could I be with these older boys? Well, the easiest way would be to earn some money and buy them beer or wine, which is what I did. It made me feel older than what I was, and I felt accepted by these older boys.

Since childhood I had felt the fear of rejection. It was a driving force in my life. I was also afraid of my father. He didn't show much feelings or love. He did in his own way, by telling me I could write well or was a good student, but it was not the kind of emotional love I was looking for.

When I got to high school age, I would sit along the wall, very silent, very isolated, but when I had a couple of beers, I was less shy. I was much more social. I felt better. I think I drank for that reason. But I think my primary reasons for drinking then was to not be a sissy and to appear older than I was.

My drinking seemed fine. I was not only relaxed but also aggressive. It went on like that through my final year of high school. I was drinking more and more but never thought I had a problem because I was a very good student, and I could manipulate my way around any situation that came up. When I went to the university, I started working during summer vacation time, as a guide for the tourists in Poland. That introduced me to various hotels. I lived in hotels during these months and would go to the bars after work, drinking more and more. I would get into quarrels or fights or do things I didn't remember.

As a student, I was dividing my time equally between the library, where I was studying very hard, and the bar next door, where I was drinking very hard. And that was my life—oscillating between these two worlds.

Because I studied a lot I had very good grades. So then, because of my good grades, I could reward myself with a drink. I was notorious for that. No one ever said I was an alcoholic, because an alcoholic would be a screwup, and I was a very good student.

After I finished school, I went to work and also started writing. By age twenty-five or twenty-six, I realized that drinking was getting in the way of my work. So I changed my work! I was employed in a publishing house as an editor. I was competent at my work, very fast, so I said to my boss that I can't come every day because I am wasting a lot of time. She agreed I could work at home. She would give me a book to edit and give me a month to do it. I would work day and night, finish in a week, and then I would binge for three weeks.

Around age twenty-six or so my entire life revolved around working and drinking. I became a writer, and my work did not interfere with my drinking. I didn't understand this pattern, but when I sobered up I realized that all my decisions—about being married or unmarried, having a relationship with someone or having no relationship with that person, choosing what kind of work to do, selecting where to live—all those decisions were driven by this internal desire to drink as much as I wanted, wherever I wanted, whenever I wanted, et cetera.

I think I was moving away all the elements in my life that were not compatible with my drinking. It was difficult to reconcile God with drinking, so I became an agnostic or an atheist—"I don't need God to understand the world." My drinking was getting incompatible with some morals that I had, so I determined I would decide about my morals because I'm so bright and intelligent. Morals were getting in the way of my emotional life and ability to love, so I put them aside and changed love into sexual adventurism and conquests.

Basically, I realized later, my sex life had little to do with love. Actually, it had little to do with sex also. I was just trying to prove to myself that someone could accept me.

That's what my sexual promiscuity was about. I was unable to make commitments, so I loved away and adopted the philosophy of a drifter as good and nice. It was like I was peeling an onion. I was left with less and less, and more and more that was compatible with my drinking became the conscious center of my life, my identity.

I got into some trouble with the police. Fighting with friends and strangers. But nothing ever came of it. No serious charges were ever filed against me, because I was from the socially "established" class. People who are educated, like me, didn't get thrown into jail or prisons. You have to kill someone to go to jail if you are from the upper classes. Jail was for the lower classes in my country.

Therefore I escaped the consequences of my drinking by various means. In time I became a writer and journalist. I had become a celebrity of sorts, and, of course, that fed into my ego and my drinking. I could say that I was just rewarding myself for all my hard work. Some people were suggesting I had a problem, but I responded by saying, "Problem? What are you talking about?" I thought I was entitled to binge once in a while because it was so difficult to turn off my brain.

Some people go to the seashore for vacation. I go to the bars.

In time, I started having more problems. Mostly with my behavior. I would get into fights and then promise myself that I would stop drinking. So I would stop but then start again after a few days.

In 1974, after a very long binge that lasted forty-two days, I got into a fight and was badly beaten. I don't remember it well; perhaps it was after a fight. I just fell into the street and injured my head. I got so scared that I went to a psychiatrist that someone had recommended to me and told him very honestly about myself. I also asked him about my drinking.

It turned into a six-hour conversation. The psychiatrist and I became very friendly. He was a very famous psychiatrist, and he said to me that I should not worry too much because, "You have such an incredible self-consciousness that you'll be OK." So I resumed drinking and drank for another nine years with self-consciousness.

This self-consciousness, however, did not prevent me from drinking. In fact, it got worse and worse. Nine years later I came to New York and saw my friend Jim Abernathy [whose story also appears in this book], and we started talking about life and drinking. He did not let me talk about my self-consciousness for six hours. In fact, after about ten minutes he stopped me and said that I should stop lying. I said, "I'm not lying to you." And he said, "No, you're not lying to me—you're lying to yourself. I know, because I lied in precisely the same way."

My life was really going downhill at this point. I spent less time working and more time bingeing. I was becoming less capable of writing. I was having more and more quarrels and fights. I was losing friends, and I was feeling ever more isolated and alone. I thought there was a beast in me that woke up when I started drinking. But I was still capable of rationalizing and finding reasons and excuses for why I could drink.

I came to the United States on December 22, 1974, to Hartford, Connecticut, to visit my friends on my way to California. There was a party that night being given by the famous American writer William Styron, whom I had previously met in Poland. I went to this party, and Styron welcomed me and asked me what I wanted to drink. Since I was dry at that time, I said, "Ginger ale," and watched as he turned to the bar to get it. I suddenly found myself absolutely enraged at him. And it wasn't until years later that I realized why. My plan was that I would tell him to get me ginger ale and he would say, "You came halfway around the world to drink ginger ale? Have some vodka or something." And I would have it, of course, because I was starved to have it and I would blame him. How could I say no to William Styron?

I was just six weeks dry at that point, and every cell in my body wanted to drink, and I was furious with William Styron for depriving me of that opportunity.

I realized that all I was thinking was basically rationalization. I was an alcoholic and I needed to have a drink without admitting that I was an alcoholic. I even went to treatment reluctantly, rationalizing it with the need to fix my liver. Fortunately, I stayed in treatment for a good reason, because I wanted to wake up every morning without fear and remorse.

And that's what I say, that good treatment, a good recovery program, or the good influence of people around a sobering alcoholic is actually changing his motivation. My original motivation was sufficient to stop drinking but was not sufficient to stay stopped. And what happened by dint of the program and my treatment was that I got motivation to stay stopped. I found a new way of living through working the twelve steps of recovery. I came into the program because I couldn't stop drinking, but I learned that my problem was me, not the drink.

About five years into my sobriety, a friend who knew me very well said, "It's very interesting. You know, Wiktor, something has happened to you. You are completely different than you were, and yet at the same time you are absolutely the same."

I did not initially understand the profundity of that, especially since it was from a friend who was still a drinking alcoholic. But then I realized that this was the case. My instincts, my reactions, my way of walking, thinking, acting were precisely as they were. But my second reaction, what to do with this feeling, was revolutionized. So if I see something that makes me indignant, I get angry. When afraid, I get panicky . . . or whatever. But whereas before I would go drink, now I do some of the constructive things that I learned in the twelve-step program.

So the core of my personality is the same, but now I am saying, "God save me from my first reaction. Let me wait until my second reaction because this will be better."

But I stopped saying that because I got confused between which is my first and which is my second. I was getting better and better, and sometimes my first reactions were turning out to be the better ones! But most of the time I hang on and the sober, better reaction makes itself evident to me and is clearly right.

But it all took time. No wonder that at the beginning of sobriety I was more miserable, mean, angry, and destructive to other people, especially to those closest around me, than ever. Probably even during drinking I was not that desperate and that bad. Because I still had all these emotions pulling me down, fears and the inability to live, and I did not have my medication, my alcohol.

At the same time, I was self-righteous. In years when I drank, many people told me how wonderful I was when I went on the wagon. So when I stopped drinking, I thought that now I was wonderful and everyone should carry me on their hands and bring me flowers and praises. And yet, some people still treated me like a bastard. How could that be?

This was when I was learning a new way of life. This process was experimental rather than intellectual. It was not that being bright and intelligent I could learn when someone told me something. I was learning primarily through crises, real experiences in my life. I could either learn something during these crises and grow or just give up and be angry. I chose to learn.

My family was falling apart and that was a crisis. I learned that I could either try to fix my family and stay miserable, or accept my family as they were and become more content.

I got into eating, a lot of overeating, and I got into a crisis with that. It had become so bad that I was forced to deal with my inner child and inner feelings that I was soothing with food.

I also got into a crisis from trying to fix my recovery group so that it would run the way I wanted it to be run. That didn't go well, so I learned to stop trying to be a leader of everything and instead become a regular member of the community.

And how this experience of sobriety deepens over time I found interesting. It has been twenty-five years now, and I have my recovery habits. I don't go often to meetings, but I do go when I am in Budapest, where I teach two months of every year. I don't speak Hungarian, and I feel lonely when I am in Budapest. Thus, the English-speaking recovery group there is like my family. It's my home group. I come once or twice a year over there, and many new people attend a meeting and I say, "You don't know me, but it's my home group." Budapest is where I get my anniversary chips.

But for twenty years, every morning wherever I am, I spend about an hour in an armchair, praying, meditating, reading books like *24 Hours a Day* and some poetry—receiving spiritual food.

And I review the steps. Because I was told that is ongoing. I do not see everything from the same angle because I try to come to them fresh. I believe that you come closest to the perception of God early in the morning, before you get crammed with daily business. So I am doing that faithfully every morning. I read passages from four or five meditation books simultaneously. And there has not been a single instance over the last ten or fifteen years when, if I had a pending problem, I didn't find a direct answer in one of the books—a direct answer!

This started precisely on December 1, 1983—eight months into my sobriety. On the way back from America to Poland, my wife and I went on a trip around Europe. That day, I woke up in Cordova in Spain, and I was just in panic, shouting.

My wife asked, "What happened?" and I said, "I had a dream that I got drunk. And they told me during my treatment that if I go on that trip, I will get drunk. I am scared."

And she said, "Calm down, you're not drunk. It's just a dream."

I said, "What are you talking about? No, I'm in grave danger."

I needed to get home immediately and demanded that we take the first flight available to Poland.

Ewe suggested that I should meditate, so I took the *24 Hours a Day* book and read the "Thought for the Day, December One": "It is a question whether or not our subconscious minds ever become entirely free from alcoholic thoughts as long as we live. For instance, some of us dream about being drunk when we are asleep. . . . But when our conscious minds are fully conditioned against drinking, we can stay sober and our subconscious minds do not often bother us."

It was just what I needed and wanted to hear. And from then on I always had coincidences like that. Whenever I had some problems I received guidance exactly pertaining to them from my reading. How is it that from recovery meditation books I find the answers to the problems that arise in my life?

This is not superstition but common sense. It is because we have only five problems, five areas we address with different certainty or insufficiency in our lives:

The problem of self-image, of ego and ambition
The problem with how we relate to God and spirituality
The problem of how we relate to other people

The problem of our fears
The problem of what gives sense and meaning to our life

Thousands of things that bother us are just different masks for these five problems. If I read the five meditation books before me I should find an answer in one of them.

So my problems are also simplified a lot.

I also developed a habit that became indispensable in my life. Someone taught me to use the feeling journal to get to know my feelings better. I did this faithfully for some time and realized that how we deal with feelings is what recovery is all about.

I realized that recovery is primarily about choosing and producing feeling with which I feel good. This is altogether different from being honest because one can be honest and still suffer a lot, for example, when one subordinates one's needs to the will or whims of other people.

To maintain a sober life it's not enough to have faith in God. I know many people who got religion and still drank after that. Many alcoholics are priests and chaplains, and so forth. They remain alcoholics, therefore God is definitely not sufficient. It's also not enough to be a good, law-abiding citizen. Many people are law-obeying yet prey to an addiction. Some criminals are sober and some law-obeying people are drunk, so it definitely doesn't work along these lines. From my feeling journal I learned what it's all about. I need God to not be alone and to have a sense of community and meaning. I need the penal code to act decently and to resist evil acts. And I need the twelve steps so that by my behavior and my thoughts I can produce feelings with which I feel well.

Recovery is about how I feel. Because if I had a conflict between what I feel and what I do, I would get drunk. But if my feelings are reconciled in myself, then I can ride the waves of my experience.

So this is about how I feel with myself, with my behavior, with my emotions, with my thoughts. Not my conscience—that is given by God—but my emotions of a lifetime like a gnarled tree.

If I want to be miserable, I will do things by which I will produce feelings of anger, jealousy, or fear. If I want to be content, I will not do things that will produce these feelings. Practicing the twelve steps was learning with what I feel good and with what I don't feel good, on a daily basis.

Being a teacher by profession, I developed a concept of a multiplier. If you have a good teacher, the multiplier is between two and three. You put one hour into learning. The good teacher will help so that you benefit as much as if you were studying by yourself for three hours—that's a multiplier of three. Some teachers in some schools, especially those who are focused on demonstrating to students what they do not know and did not learn—the multiplier is half. By myself I will learn much more than with that lousy teacher.

The twelve-step recovery program is a teaching program with a multiplier of ten. This is incredible because you put effort and you get ten times more. Of learning programs known to me it is the most efficient. The virtues of this program are due to how it addresses identity, identification, community, feedback, and also experiential learning by consequences and honesty with admitting responsibility.

However, ten multiplied by zero is still zero. If you don't put in work, you will have zero. If you put in work, you get ten times more. This is what the program I follow is—it's not a miracle, you have to put in work, but you will see incredible results.

# 12

# Johnny Allem

*Although people who have recovered stay out of society's sight because they think it's safer, this contributes to the growing mythology that alcoholics and addicts are not moral individuals.*

—JOHNNY ALLEM, "ADDICTION: IT'S A SECRET
WE CAN'T AFFORD TO KEEP"

Beginning as a newspaper reporter in Knoxville, Tennessee, in 1956, Johnny Allem established a Florida public relations firm in the 1960s, a Washington political consulting firm in the 1970s, and a printing company in the 1980s. He is also the former president of the Johnson Institute, a noted Washington, D.C.–based nonprofit in the substance abuse advocacy field.

Allem went from press secretary for Senator Vance Harte of Indiana in 1969–1970 to political campaign consulting, and he garnered a reputation as a real firecracker in that career. Between 1971 and 1980 he provided management and consulting services for more than a hundred campaigns for the U.S. Senate, U.S. House of Representatives, governors, mayors, state political parties, and labor organizations. He designed grassroots systems for the Clinton-Gore campaign in 1992.

Besides working as an independent, Allem held pivotal positions in D.C. government, where he was director of communications and also director of operations of the Department of Mental Health Services. In 1972 Allem created the PEOPLE political action training program for the American Federation of State, County, and Municipal Employees union that has graduated more than forty thousand union members.

Throughout his more than twenty-five years in recovery, Allem has worked to advance solutions to drug and alcohol abuse. He worked with the late Senator Harold Hughes as executive director of the Society of Americans in Recovery; served on the planning committee for the 2001 summit that organized Faces and Voices in Recovery; and organized recovery clubs within the District of Columbia. As a District of Columbia official from 1995 to 2002, he authorized the first elementary school program to offer mental health counseling to students and pioneered the district's first training program to address individuals with co-occurring addiction and mental illness.

Allem received his master's in journalism and public affairs at American University in Washington, D.C., in 1999. His daughter, Janet, is a financial officer with the U.S. Agency for International Development, and his son, John, now runs the D.C. printing enterprise his father founded. Allem's wife, Barbara, is retired from a career with the U.S. Senate. They reside in Washington, D.C., within easy visiting distance of their three grandchildren.

# JOHNNY ALLEM

I am a very loved person today.

My immediate and extended family is in my life almost daily. I count several loving networks of friends and family throughout the greater Washington area—former customers, fellow D.C.

government workers, community and political activists, and those sharing my recovery journey. Across America I enjoy friendships from countless political endeavors, organizing campaigns, policy causes, and the recovery community.

This huge payoff from life is a direct result of wisdom given to me by others. Find the joy of loving both individual people and humanity in general, and place no conditions on either. And start by giving yourself a break. Today, I love me to the core.

My daily prayer is to express gratitude for God's love as expressed to me through people and for the good sense to pass love on as it is so freely delivered to me.

If this sounds too Pollyanna, let me share that all this peace goes away in a heartbeat when I fail to feed my spiritual condition. But I know that as long as I do, the peace will continue—for me and for everyone else who does the work.

It was not always so. I was raised with conditional love. Growing up, I had to earn it. And the conditions were steep and often elusive.

I'm the oldest of seven children and the only boy—I have six sisters. My father was a fundamental evangelist in small-town east Tennessee. He believed in a very vengeful God and a very narrow salvation. I grew up resisting that message. My grandfather was a moral man, and he also happened to be an alcoholic. He quit drinking during Prohibition, because he didn't want to break the law, and started drinking a few days after its repeal. I'm sure he planned to quit again, someday, but the beast had awakened, and he could not put it back to sleep. He drank until he lost his job, his home, and eventually his life.

His sons watched this and all three, including my father, became preachers and lifelong abstainers. They kept most of this story from me as a child, perhaps out of shame. I grew up and went into business, and though I consider myself a moral man, I, too, would become an alcoholic. I, too, would experience loss of control, blackouts, and altered behavior almost from the beginning. I would spend over two decades trying to drink like other folks until I was lucky enough to run into a group of people who taught me that alcoholism is a disease from which you can recover. Otherwise I'm sure I would have followed in my grandfather's footsteps.

As a youngster I was active in church, singing with my sisters in a Gospel trio. I was more comfortable with messages of love and caring, as opposed to messages of fear, loss, and eternal punishment. In time, I tended to rebel against my father and his religious views. I practiced a belief in a God of mercy and a spiritual life based on love, kindness, and salvation. I continued to teach Sunday school at a Knoxville street-front church after I left home. As I grew in my newspaper career, however, I pretty much lost that early religious zeal.

I did not drink when I was young. Mostly, I think, because I played basketball from sixth grade on—nearly a religion in the Tennessee Valley at the time. It also helped that I did not grow up near my relatives, many of whom died terrible alcoholic deaths. It seems that addiction was part of our family history for generations. As best I can determine, I am the first in my father's family tree to achieve sobriety and recovery.

We lived in very modest circumstances, so going to college was not a given. Fortunately, my high school librarian loaned me a hundred dollars and spurred me to register at a college. I hitchhiked from Dayton, Tennessee, to Knoxville, and registered at the University of Tennessee. Tuition for one quarter was $104, so I was four dollars in the hole.

I had been a sports and county correspondent in my county for the *Chattanooga News-Free Press* during high school. Needing a job to pay for school, I took my clippings to the *Knoxville Journal*, and within a day I became a cub reporter. I was seventeen years old.

Although I started college with an aim to be an electrical engineer, within a couple of years, I became more interested in writing and being a reporter, so I dropped out of school.

Looking back, I had done a lot of things growing up that I should be proud of; however, I never saw myself as being successful. I always felt I was not reaching the bar. In high school I was a writer; I sold stories successfully. I was co-captain of my basketball team. I learned how to wire houses and got licensed as an electrician. TV installations with giant roof-top antenna arrays were big then, and I am still remembered for climbing tin roofs all over Rhea County. I even owned a gas station for a while in Knoxville. I was enterprising, always into something—sometimes things finished well and sometimes they didn't. But I always felt a little "less than."

Working in the newsroom, learning the discipline of reporting before you write, and seeing my work printed every day gave me a new sense of career and calling. I loved the contact with new things, the chance to follow my curiosity, and being educated by reporting on real life. I found my space in the universe.

I moved from cub reporter status to night police reporter. I was offered a job with the Associated Press, which I certainly should have taken, but it was too scary and intimidating for me. Instead I began reporting feature stories as well as covering my police beat. As a police reporter, I made strong friendships with the emergency room nurses at all the Knoxville hospitals. My first wife was the sister of the head nurse at the University of Tennessee hospital. She worked in a doctor's office but would come over to see her sister after work. She accepted a dare to squirt me with a water gun when I came into the ER.

I was getting some static from my father, who was trying to reestablish a relationship with me. We had not had much more than a speaking relationship. I simply could not forgive his treatment of me growing up. My anger stemmed more from the unyielding disapproval than the savage beatings when he lost his temper. He was sure of his knowledge of God's will. It was so difficult for him to allow his oldest child and only son to find a path to adulthood by trial and error. The beatings stopped when I was ten. I refused to cry or make a sound. He beat me until I crumbled on the floor. He left the house and never touched me again. (I very lately have come to see his anger spells and abuse as symptoms of being a child of an alcoholic. His untreated condition resulted in a very unhappy life.)

My escape to the university was really to get away from home. My father had gotten a job in Knoxville and wanted to come back in my life—but only on his religious terms. I wasn't up for that.

When I got married, we wasted no time in trying to start a family. I was twenty and my wife was nineteen. I quit my newspaper job and we moved to Florida, primarily to lose contact with my father. I didn't see my family for many years.

In Florida I shifted through several jobs—I worked for Delta Airlines for a while, sold Fuller Brushes, worked as a private detective, and did travel sales—before settling into writing again. I wound up writing, often in a political vein, as I had loved politics since high school and remained connected with it my entire life.

By this time I was twenty-two years old, we had two children, and I worked for an advertising agency, while keeping up my writing on the side. I was not the most outgoing kind of person, but I could write well and had a knack for designing ads that worked for the clients. I tried to avoid the social affairs and receptions that went along with the ad business.

My first drink was at one of those receptions. There was a highball bar right at the door so guests could help themselves. It never occurred to me to drink. I don't know why. But one night I did. I like to remember that there was no causality except maybe boredom because nothing unusual or particularly trying was going on then in my life.

But I picked up a drink and discovered that I had all the right equipment to be an alcoholic: my arm bent in the middle.

For the first time in my life, I became comfortable in my own skin. It was a marvelous experience. I discovered what was missing in my life—and we all know the story there!

Within a few minutes, I had two or three more highballs. I began a routine I was to perfect for the next twenty-two years: I got drunk. I had a blackout. I fell down. And someone had to come and get me. But I knew the next morning that I had found the magic. I just had to polish it up a little bit.

Within a few months I was drinking alcoholically and having blackouts. I stayed pretty successful at my work. I was deeply motivated to build our young family, and that carried me along. I soon opened my own agency.

In my advertising and marketing agency, I became known for teaching home builders how to sell real estate door-to-door. I had been a Fuller Brush salesman, and I adapted door-to-door selling to new home marketing. Using my "show-and-tell" sales tools and city buses chartered to take families to barbeques on Saturday, we moved a lot of center-city residents to new homes in the suburbs in the 1960s.

I had three clients in Florida, all of whom went out of business when the housing market collapsed in 1966. I was in sore straits and began to work full time in politics. I had worked in various election campaigns and also freelanced as a sound technician for Movietone News while working in advertising and public relations. As a sound man, I covered Cape Canaveral and the space station and got to know John Glenn and Walter Cronkite, along with a lot of other folks who came down for the space launches there. Because of my airline experience, I also ran the "pool" film shuttle. This meant picking up film from all the network crews after the space shot, jumping into a stand-by Cessna, then flying to either Orlando or Jacksonville. In those days, I handed the orange bags directly to an airline captain. A pool messenger would meet the flight in New York and rush the film to processing before the evening news.

By 1967 both agency and freelance opportunities diminished and politics offered me the full-time job I needed.

I became a speech writer and communications director for LeRoy Collins, a former governor of Florida. He became my political mentor. The first nonsegregationist Southern governor, he ran for the U.S. Senate in 1968 as one of the first leaders to oppose the Vietnam War. That did not lead to his winning the Senate race, but the experience put me on a new, full-time path in organizing grassroots activists and managing political campaigns. The climate for someone with my liberal beliefs was rather thin in Florida, however, so my friends advised me to move someplace more progressive.

So I came to Washington in 1969 and began handling campaigns all over the South and Midwest. It was the very beginning of the political consulting business, and I was one of the pioneers. I traveled the country and was going to save the world in my blue jeans, with long hair and plenty of Jim Beam. I had a good time and did a lot of interesting things. My wife and two children soon adjusted to the D.C.-Virginia suburbs and to my travels.

A good campaign manager is the ultimate entrepreneur. You have to think strategically and act tactically on a moment-by-moment basis, never forgetting your primary goals. It requires great stamina, tact, leadership, and humility. I think that it is one of the great leadership training grounds available to young people who have a passion for democracy and team effort.

I worked as management or in a major consulting role in more than one hundred campaigns and loved every minute. In the early days of consulting, I was not well known in the press but was considered a top "fire engine" guy who could turn things around on a minimum budget. I also worked with unions and associations, primarily AFSCME, the American Federation of State, County,

and Municipal Employees, where I crafted their very successful
political action training in 1972 and 1973.

I was drunk a lot during this period of my life. I drank steadily. I
would drink Monday to Friday. When I was home on the weekend
with my wife and children I didn't have the need for my "medicine" like I did while working. So while I was a big Monday to
Friday drunk, I was not a big weekend drinker.

Overall, the work went well. Public employees were just beginning to be active then. I got to be part of their spectacular story. I
did some other interesting things, such as writing campaign hand-
books for the Democratic National Committee.

Alcohol was taking its toll on my personal life, however. My
marriage turned pretty sour after we moved to Washington. This
was largely due to my drinking, and we divorced in 1972, after
fifteen years of marriage and two children.

Though I know I disappointed them time after time, I tried my
best to keep up a good relationship with my children. They were
really my enablers, my loyal children who always stood up for me
and pretended to understand when things got rough. I already
knew I was drinking too much but didn't know what to do about
it. I knew that I needed to self-medicate; alcohol was the medicine
that kept me going. Even though I wound up in serious difficulties, like missed deadlines, canceled contracts, or angry clients, it
was just a requirement of life like food, and I wasn't about to stop
eating, and I wasn't about to stop drinking—or breathing. They
all went together for me. But it became clear that the huge capacity for drinking I demonstrated for many years melted away before
I was thirty-three, leaving alcohol in charge and me sucking air
most of the time. I began to hate what I had become and worked
hard to be alone with my bottle. Instead of drinking to feel connected, I cut connections to drink alone.

Politics are a particular "scene" from the perspective of intoxi-
cants. A political campaign is a fascinating "culture on the run."

There is a work-hard, play-hard mentality that is very enticing. It is very hard work. Very demanding. You produce or you are out. Overall, people enter this game because they are highly motivated and have strong beliefs about America and its future. The pace and the climate are conducive to living large, including drinking and chasing the opposite sex to excess. And, of course, there are always a few players who are simply playing for personal motives and have no principles.

For me, drinking was a necessity. I thought I worked best when my chemistry was right. I know today that my creativity is not necessarily enhanced by alcohol. But I labored with a buzz on throughout the campaign season. I delivered well, though I also produced some highly embarrassing moments.

There is a lot more money in campaigns today. A lot more. With campaign teams and consultants, so much money is at stake that the Wild West climate I operated in is not tolerated as much.

Young people with alcoholic tendencies do well in the business because of the high tolerance for drinking that occurs early in the illness cycle. We do crash, however, and I eventually had to get out before I was thrown out.

I hadn't crashed yet, so for me, that lifestyle went on and on . . . and on. I really wanted to stop drinking and thought if I stopped traveling and got out of politics I could do that. So I went into the printing business two blocks from the White House. I was also introduced to a twelve-step program. I had married again and went to a meeting with my wife and a family friend, who was trying very hard to get sober. Her doctor had suggested it, and I think I went along out of curiosity as much as to support our friend.

When I got to that first meeting, I felt completely at home. It felt like a safe place for me, although I wasn't about to stop drinking. They talked about peace and spirituality in a way that was completely different from the religion of my father. It was very comfortable. So I would go to meetings once a week or so and try to figure this all out. This went on for nearly a year.

My last drink was at a political event. I walked into a fund-raiser and someone gave me a glass of vodka. I promptly drank it—and two more. I don't know what happened next, but I was told I got into a fight with a national reporter and made a general ass out of myself. I woke up the next morning and something deep inside me said, "You need to go back to those meetings and do what they say and stop thinking so much."

That was March 23, 1982, and since then I don't drink.

So my recovery began—at least the physical recovery. My printing business would get steadier as I steadied, but not for a while. I was still losing money hand over fist. But it got better like I did: one day at a time.

My son and I kind of grew up together in the printing business. He was twenty-one and I was forty-three when we founded the company. I got sober the next year, when I was forty-four. We sold it in 1991. He is still in the printing trade, widely respected and well liked in the D.C. printing industry. I am pretty visionary, but he is really a better manager. I guess if he picked anything up from me it is my belief that family is everything and to treat everyone like family.

I married Barbara, my present wife, in 1976. She worked in the Senate, becoming the first female chief clerk of the Senate Foreign Relations Committee. Barbara was, and is, instrumental in my sobriety. She is retired now and enjoys her family twelve-step fellowship, painting, gardening, and grandchildren. My son and daughter have always been my best friends. They are part of my story at every stage. They have lived with their mother and with me at different times. Both were active in high school band, as I was.

My daughter earned a scholarship to Barnard in New York and later got a master's in finance at George Washington University here in D.C. She followed me in politics, however, holding a number of major management jobs in campaigns in the eighties and nineties. While heading the state Democratic effort in Illinois in 1992, she was diagnosed with multiple sclerosis. This curtailed her political work. After a difficult few years, she stabilized and became financial officer for USAID. Today, she is a single mother of an adopted Cambodian "princess," now nine years old.

I couldn't have been happier than when I sold the printing business press in 1991. It was very satisfying to have turned it around and done rather well financially. I had learned that you don't always make it on the daily work but on the value of the business overall. We had a very good sale that allowed me to be more choosey about the rest of my life.

During that period, from my getting sober in 1982 to 1992, I did very little in politics. I remained on the District Democratic Committee here and had a couple friends I worked for, most notably Max Cleland, a personal friend as well as client, in Georgia. Other than that I really had stayed clear of the kind of political involvement that marked my early life. I believed it was a slippery place for me, and I really didn't want to drink again. In 1985 I served as chair of the Mayor's Committee on Alcoholism. But I didn't regard that as being involved in politics.

In 1992 a couple of things happened to call me back to policy and politics. I became close to retired U.S. Senator Howard Hughes, who was responsible for the Hughes Act, in which the U.S. government first recognized addiction and recovery. He formed an organization called Society of Americans for Recovery (SOAR). His message was that those of us in recovery had to find our voices and claim our citizenship. I became executive director of SOAR.

SOAR was not received very well. In fact, it was just terribly frustrating, because Americans didn't want to hear our message. The nation's answer to the addiction epidemic was to engage in the largest jail-building spree in the history of civilization. People in recovery were fearful of speaking out—because of real discrimination on the job as well as very narrow interpretations of anonymity traditions. And there was absolutely no money for such a cause.

But I also became involved in Bill Clinton's campaign for president, doing a number of chores that included designing a national grassroots system and producing state and regional campaign literature. This was my first paid political job in recovery. I was just amazed. I could practice my old trade and I was still good at it. And I did not get drunk. That was a real discovery.

Along with other consulting work, I renewed my interest and work in local politics, becoming director of communications for the district government, then deputy commissioner of mental health.

Along the way I learned a couple of things: Number one, that I could do the work and not drink. Number two, that I could apply in the public sector what I had practiced in the private sector. I was a good business manager and was responsible for the business side of the mental health department. I directed the operations of a 2,600-employee agency with a $360 million budget for the District of Columbia for five years. While that was my day job, I stayed in service in the recovery community, working to get treatment for the growing homeless population in D.C.

In my day job at the mental health department, I was able to see how lack of citizen support hampered any effort to make the agency more responsive to problems of alcohol and other drugs. If you didn't have people out there supporting you, a city agency couldn't do very much. And at that time addiction services had very little public support—nobody gave a damn about it! And people in recovery stayed firmly in the closet.

In my volunteer time I also worked with the Johnson Institute. They were finding ways to do what Hughes had begun: to mobilize the recovery community and build public awareness that recovery was the solution. These efforts led up finally to the Faces and Voices of Recovery, a national advocacy agency, funded by the Johnson Institute.

When William Cope Moyers resigned as president of the Johnson Institute in 2001, I had just retired from district government and was happy to accept the organization's offer to replace him. I recently retired after six years as president-CEO. It has been a rewarding journey, and I believe we have strengthened the voice of recovery in America.

That's my career in a nutshell. I've always been reasonably ethical. I told my kids growing up, "It isn't a moral thing, it's just good business to be honest. It's bad business to get enmeshed in lies." So I've never known how to cheat at business and make it work. What fettered my accomplishments was not knowing who I was—overpromising, making promises I couldn't keep, and undervaluing my capacity, or staying power. None of these were good business traits.

I have always known that integrity is the best business practice. My recovery program has helped me execute that value, primarily by living in the now. My experience in recovery also taught me to value myself better and not give away either my knowledge or my time. If you take care of business and are consistent about it, success always follows. Working the steps, for me, is taking care of business.

Another lesson I remember is to be a little broader about my definition of success. I have made lots of money and lost lots of money. My therapist said that the reason I'm not rich is that money is not important to me, and I guess maybe that's true.

In recovery I've sorted that out. I'm not the wealthiest guy on the block, but we have a place to stay, and God has been very good to me materially. I went through most of my life never taking vacations. I take vacations now. I have season tickets to the symphony orchestra. My wife loves baseball and I go to baseball games. That's part of taking care of business.

There's a section in an affirmation book I read that is about working with a sharp knife. That's a business concept that is meaningful to me. Working with a dull knife we kind of make a dull mess. That's why meditation, rest, exercise, regular diet, going to twelve-step meetings, and volunteering for others is "taking care of business."

At the same time, I take care of business associated with my passion for recovery—that the opportunity for recovery will someday reach every person on Earth who needs it. I wrote a book with Trish Merrill called *Healing Places*. It is the story of Faith Partners, the congregational team ministry she developed in Texas and Oklahoma with a little Johnson Institute funding. My part has been to craft a business plan to spread this powerful idea across America. Today seventeen faith traditions use this model in twelve states.

I am so proud of Trish and this work. It has the potential to reach so many people before they reach the kind of crisis that I did.

If I had to put my business principles in the simplest form, it would be:

1. I am not in charge.
2. That's a good thing.
3. I function best when I keep my recovery first.
4. I keep my recovery first by service.

I believe that just as money is the currency of material life, love is the currency of spiritual life. The God of my understanding is the source of this currency, and I take care of business by being a channel of God's love, letting as much as possible flow through me and to others.

In this, I know I am loved—even by myself.

# 13

# Marius Hickman

*He loved being happy! He loved happiness like*
*I love tea.*

—Eudora Welty, *The Ponder Heart*

Marius Hickman was born in the town of Border, Texas, in the late 1960s. Raised mostly in Tulsa, Oklahoma, he went to Houston with his mother and sister when his parents divorced, and there he finished high school. Dancing was his first love; he danced informally from earliest childhood. To study dance, and get away from home (where he felt he had to stand in for the father in a family he helped support in his teen years), he moved to Ithaca, New York. Now Marius was free to express and try out his different talents. In Ithaca and New York City he studied ballet and jazz, dancing for the next ten years, six hours a day. Currently, he lives in Venice, California—"I live a few blocks from the ocean, and walking by the beach soothes me after a day of baking. As a Pisces I'm ruled by Neptune."

Everything Marius does he does with a passion and effervescent energy, yet when you speak with him you are aware of his consciousness of keeping it smooth and low key. He loves to eat and cook, averring, "I like being around people and I love to cook. Nothing is better than a good meal and good company. This is what makes life tolerable. . . . Even a simple thirty-minute meal, because I love the act of getting ingredients and anticipation of what they will become."

His business is cookies, and the cookies Southern California clamors for in particular are his chocolate chunk pecans. His kitchen, Marius Morsels, also makes specialty varieties like a Hawaii-inspired recipe on commission for a Hawaiian client. In Marius's view the baking is a science, and his success derives from systemization, goals, and anticipating so the business grows but he is never in crisis mode. His immediate goal is to bake 100,000 cookies a month.

In his off-hours, he turns to gardening and painting (he meditates first) because the day's work goes better. He is also an animal lover. "Animals tune me into spirit quickly. My Italian greyhound and I are connected where we can sense each other's feelings and thoughts."

Someday he plans to resume dancing, which he credits with the physical stamina and training in discipline he draws on to carry out the rigors of baking.

Meanwhile, despite the intense occupation, Marius treats all day—working, being by himself, and being around people—as fun. "The things I love to do are all fun things, aren't they?" he says. "I live my life with fun."

---

## MARIUS HICKMAN

I thought from the very beginning that the world was against me, and I had to constantly prove myself. As a result, I always came up short.

I was a person sitting on a fence watching life go by, thinking, "Wouldn't it be better if . . .?" (Maybe, "Wouldn't it be better if I were taller?" Or, "Wouldn't it be better if I had long hair, or if

I made more money?") I never gave myself a fair shake because I didn't know how to. I was raised with the belief that if you work hard, you'll have rewards. So I would work hard but never get there.

As a young man I wanted to be a dancer. I spent a lot of time studying but rarely auditioned for jobs, because I never felt I was good enough. I thought I was too short, or too effeminate, or there was always someone better. Ultimately, I stopped going to auditions altogether and took a job waiting tables in a restaurant.

I had worked since I was seven years old. All the money I ever made went to help support my family, because my father was an alcoholic, an untreated alcoholic, and was not really around. I was raised in the South—Texas, to be exact—and my parents were high school sweethearts. After five years of marriage their relationship was in trouble, but they didn't separate. Suffice it to say, they didn't offer a good example of how to have a healthy relationship. What they taught me was stick with your partner no matter what, and don't change. I'm not blaming my parents. I really don't want to say that my life would have been better "if only."

At any rate, I didn't achieve any of the things that I wanted to achieve. I blamed all the outer circumstances instead of seeing there was something in me that needed to change. I was the one that decided not to go to auditions. I have to take responsibility for that.

It was around this time that I discovered alcohol. I didn't start drinking until I was twenty-one. It helped me deal with my anger and disappointments: they all seemed to disappear when I drank. Working in a restaurant made it easy for me to drink after work. One drink would quickly turn to two, and I was never a person who sipped my drinks. I would drink very fast. About three drinks is what it took for me to start feeling comfortable and to have a conversation with people.

I just thought that that's what adults did. I never realized that I wasn't drinking responsibly. I didn't even know that you could drink responsibly. I thought the reason to drink was to get out of myself, and I liked that. Needless to say, my drinking progressed to where I would get drunk, go out and meet a boyfriend, and eventually end up home alone with a turkey sandwich and some Häagen-Dazs.

Isolation—I couldn't understand why that was happening, but the truth was that no one wanted to be around me. I was a slobbering drunk yet never saw myself as that. I thought an alcoholic was someone who hid booze, a person who shook, a person who lived on the streets—and I wasn't any of those things. I was making a decent living and was able to function in society.

I worked several jobs in Ithaca over a number of years. I lived in nice houses, shopped in the right stores, ate in good restaurants, and had the right friends, although my friends were never really my friends because I didn't let them get to know me.

Eventually, I moved to New York, where some of my friends there told me I should go into rehab. I asked them why. And they said, "Because you're an alcoholic and you have a bad drinking problem." I told them I was not an alcoholic. I didn't get it, but I wanted to prove them wrong. This is how, through the grace of God, I was able to get some sober time together. But I don't really know if I was really sober, because my life didn't change and the only thing different was I was going to twelve-step recovery meetings and I wasn't drinking. But I wasn't having any spiritual experiences. That's what's different about my life today; it's filled with spiritual experiences, and that's what keeps me from drinking.

In my recovery program, they talk about having an unmanageable life, and I thought that meant having too many things to do. I didn't understand that my life itself was unmanageable. That there would constantly be things that came my direction—challenges that would require a healthy core self and test my serenity. I questioned the sober identify, asking myself, "Can I not drink through all that?" "Can I not drink when things are really good?" "Can I not drink when things are challenging?" For me, I would drink when it was a good day, and I'd drink when it was a bad day. I just liked the effect of drinking. I'd look forward to the end of my shift at work so I could have a drink. In California I couldn't wait for "Happy Hour."

So, anyway, it was at this point in New York that things really fell apart. I started losing things. Losing money, losing places to live, losing my ability to pay my bills. After a while I was pretty much living hand-to-mouth. I couldn't understand what was going on. I'd promise myself, "I'm not going to drink tonight," then I'd get off work and the next thing I knew I was in a bar and coming home drunk with no money. And I couldn't stop.

I didn't know that I had lost all control. I was still not able to see my alcoholic disease working in me. Ultimately, I got to a place where my fabulous apartment was gone; I was living in a basement flat on the upper West Side, me and my dog. One day I looked at myself in the mirror and saw that I was dying. In that moment I asked God to help me. I told him, "I can't do it anymore."

Help came with the realization that I needed to leave New York. I had been living there for eighteen years, and I realized that trying to get sober in New York wouldn't work. I had already tried that. So, I thought I should be in an environment that was sunny and warm, and sure enough, I ended up moving to Venice, California. I had never been there before, but I told God that I'd like to live by a beach, and he moved me 150 feet from the ocean, to this nice little apartment. I moved to California with four dollars in my pocket, but I never went hungry. That was a miracle.

It was also the first time that God had answered my prayers. The first day I arrived in Venice I found my way to a twelve-step meeting, which was my real start in recovery. I had gotten a little sober time, but being an alcoholic, things would hurt my feelings every now and again, and I'd drink over them. I stopped going to meetings and started drinking more and more. The unique thing was that everything that used to take a long time to happen—for instance, losing an apartment or losing a job—now all started happening really quick. I stayed away from meetings, though, and tried to get sober on my own. It worked for a little bit, but I would get to the point where I couldn't stay stopped, and once I had that first drink I was off to the races again. I thought I would have one beer, but I'd end up drinking three six-packs. And I'd hoped all that would end in the sunshine of Southern California.

Ultimately I ended up losing that Venice apartment and a friend let me stay at her house. I called it the tree house, because it was an Air Stream trailer suspended on the second floor deck of a carport, attached to a eucalyptus tree. I thought I was going to be there for ten days or so, but I lived there for over a year.

In the process of all this a business was born. It had started by accident while I was still living in New York. I was in therapy, not satisfied with my life, and my therapist asked me what did I like to do. I told her that I liked to dance and bake cookies. She suggested to me that I try to make cookies. I responded that no one will buy my cookies. Well time passed and the holiday season was upon us and I had a few friends over for dinner. The dinner was a big success, but there were no leftovers. A friend of mine saw these cookies sitting on my counter and asked for some to take home. I had never given out cookies before, because I felt like no one would like them.

He pleaded I give him some, and the next morning he called me and asked for more, and the next day he asked for more, and finally he offered to pay for them. One day I was on the subway, overwhelmed by the chaos of my life. I happened to reach into my bag and found one of the cookies I had made. I ate it, and as I was eating it all of my stress seemed to melt away. I believed if I could somehow package these cookies it could help a lot of people. I understood that there are a lot of people rushing through life for a finish line that isn't there. My idea was to get people to slow down and savor the moments.

So I meditated to find how to put everything together. I searched for the right ingredients, and once those things came together, I thought I needed to get written up, so I dropped some cookies off to the *New York Times*. To my surprise, they wrote a great little article about me and the cookies, and that is how the business was born.

So while I was living in that Air Stream, I started baking cookies again, which I was selling from out of the house. My friend had three ovens in her kitchen, and that's where I did my baking. The cookies were selling well and I was happy. Around this time I also started getting humble. I started praying to God for help.

One day I was at a twelve-step meeting and a guy came up to me and said, "I've heard you share before and something is not happening. You are not getting the message," and then he gave me this prayer: "God, please give me the grace to admit to my innermost self that I'm an alcoholic." I ended up saying that prayer 650 times that very day!

Someone else came into my life shortly thereafter and noticed the same thing. He said to me, "It's really a shame you are not getting this thing that can save your life." I never thought I was dying because of alcoholism. I thought I was dying because of my inability to make a living. I just didn't put it together, that alcohol was killing me. So this guy said to me, "If you want, I will take you through the twelve steps," and I said, "I would love it if you would do that." No one had ever done that with me. So as we started working the steps, I began to really see myself and the grave nature of my illness. I began to see that I have an obsession of the mind, born from a spiritual malady, which drives me to a drink, and, once I drink, I end up with a craving that brings me to a place where I drink more than I should. More than I intended to drink.

No wonder I have twenty drinks. No wonder ten drinks don't get me drunk, and some days one drink would put me in a black-out. It was a big turning point for me.

My world started to change. I was experiencing a psychic change. All my ideas were getting turned upside-down. Something was happening to me internally.

I give a lot of credit to the guys who introduced me to that prayer and took me through the steps. I learned what turmoil I suffer from my disease and how hopeless it is unless I change.

My experience going through the steps has been absolutely life-altering. I learned that my greatest character defect was my inability to live with the truth. My truth is that I'm OK, and there is a God who loves me beyond my wildest imagination.

If I could live with the truth there would never be any need for me to manipulate, for me to lie, for me to control or to try to make anything happen.

I remember one day I was home getting ready to deliver some of my cookies, when I heard a voice that said to me, "Sit down." But I went over to the oven to pick up the cookies and they were real heavy. Heavier than I had ever felt them before. And I heard the voice again, and it simply said, "Sit down." So I sat down and I stayed in the house for one week! I hardly ate—a little shrimp fried rice is all. It took me three days to eat a single portion. My body was on fire. I felt like I was being downloaded with information. This energy was living within me and letting itself be known. My room was filled with the smell of roses, a smell I had never smelled before. A thick, sweet smell. So thick I could taste it. You know what was weird? My phone rings often, but that week I got no calls. Well, maybe three. One from my mom, one from my sponsor, and I don't recall the third. That first night I got about twenty minutes of sleep, but it felt like eight hours. And I came through that experience a free man.

Things are significantly different today. I feel like I'm in a flow. I'm aware today that when I experience something painful, it's an opportunity for me to look at something. I certainly didn't set out to think this way. It's all a result of my newfound faith. You know, I was always looking for something like this—a spiritual existence. Now it's part of who I am. My business is thriving today. I found a man from Texas. He actually lives twenty-seven miles from where I was born. A businessman who made it, just like me. He's a real mover. One day he just showed up. He's going to help me take my business to the next level. He's a man of vision. A man who knows how to do it. He's not just in it for the money and I'm not either. I've been baking cookies before I had any money. I did it for the joy of it. I always knew I would make money doing this, but I also knew that I could bring joy to a lot of people. We should all get to live this life to the fullest.

I believe life should be enjoyed, and there should be no scrimping. In my sobriety there isn't Puritanical self-denial. The inebriated life isn't living it up—that deadens the senses. My journey has taught me you can both be sober and celebrate luxury, pleasure, and the life of the senses. Only if you are sober can you do what you aim to do before you get to the other side. My philosophy of life is in the cookie, and I want mine to have that comfort thing that hits the heart.

# 14

# Walter Yetnikoff

*An addict's best hope for recovery is being an intolerable*
*asshole when he's using.*

—"Untitled Heath Ledger Project,"
New York magazine

Walter Yetnikoff was born in the Brownsville section of
Brooklyn to a working-class Jewish family. An outstanding student, he won scholarships to both college and law school.
His first job out of Columbia Law School in 1961 was as a junior
lawyer at Rosenman & Colin, the law firm that represented CBS
Records. Not long after, he joined the CBS Records law department, which he soon headed. In 1975 he was promoted to the
chief of CBS Records, a position he held until 1990.

In the course of that career Yetnikoff became a legendary
figure—the ultimate corporate mogul in the high-stakes music
business. Then he became the epitome of someone corrupted
by power, who, when the old life toppled, struck out on a new,
enlightened path.

The eighties were the heyday of the record industry, and CBS
under Yetnikoff increased its revenues from $485 million to more
than $2 billion per annum. He was a very powerful man who
exacted equally powerful emotions of love and hate in his world.

He was the epitome of the high-powered executive, known for his tough manner, frankness, and high living, his extraordinary instincts for nurturing new talent, and his business acumen. Among the clients whose careers he nurtured were Michael Jackson, Bruce Springsteen, Barbra Streisand, Paul Simon, and Billy Joel.

Renowned for his colorful personality and his abrasive management style, Yetnikoff was a key protagonist of the 1990 book *Hit Men: Powerbrokers and Fast Money Inside the Music Business*, Frederic Dannen's exposé of the shady dealings by major American record labels in the 1970s and 1980s. The book focused on the record companies' controversial connections with "the Network," a loose grouping of so-called indies (independent record promoters) who were, by the 1980s, being paid tens of millions of dollars annually by major record labels to promote new releases to American radio stations and who could reputedly make or break a new record.

In the book, Dannen recounted Yetnikoff's rise to power at CBS; his virulent competition with his corporate rival, the Warner Music Group; and his escalating conflict with CBS Records' deputy president, Dick Asher—who came to oppose the use of indie promoters—which culminated in Yetnikoff's controversial sacking of Asher in 1983. Yetnikoff was rumored to be the inspiration for Walter Fox, the record label boss played by Rip Torn in the film *One Trick Pony*, written and directed by Paul Simon.

Yetnikoff left his job at CBS/Sony because, as he says, he was "ceremoniously canned" (typically calling a spade a spade). In the two decades since, he has reshaped his life. He wrote a no-holds-barred memoir entitled *Howling at the Moon* (2004). He volunteers at recovery centers all around New York and New Jersey. He is, as you will see in his story, just as brash and outspoken, but a man whose appetites are under control, whose power comes from within, and who is enjoying life without the notorious ego.

After leaving Sony, Yetnikoff put together the independent label Velvel Records, which debuted in 1995. The label (sold to

Koch Records in 1999) released many records under Yetnikoff's aegis, including the Kinks catalog. Subsequently, he cofounded Commotion Records, an independent label focusing on soundtrack CDs.

## WALTER YETNIKOFF

I grew up in the Brownsville section of Brooklyn in 1933, which I'm reluctant to admit. I'm sort of a Depression and early WWII kid. My mother lived a surrogate life through me—she saw me as her key out of the Brooklyn ghetto. My father was a housepainter for the Department of Hospitals. He was vicious and violent but not a drunk. My mother once told my father, "You know, your son is too smart for you. There is nothing you can teach him." So I lost a father, and he lost a son.

In any event, I carried out my mother's dictates. I went to law school, and I became successful. I rose to the top of the music part of the entertainment business and was the president of CBS/Sony Records. I was running a very large company, drugging and drinking excessively, and I got crazier and crazier. I kept hearing a voice that said, "What do you want, Walter? *What do you want?*" To which I answered, "I want peace of mind." But I was doing everything to not have peace of mind.

I was very power driven—"I am the captain of my ship and I am the master of my soul." Power is what I was really after; I wanted it more than anything else. More than money. Not that I was antimoney. I was just following my mother's dictates: "If you have money, you have power"—also not true.

What's that expression? "It's more important to want what you have than get what you want." I wanted power, and I got what I wanted. But it almost killed me. So this went on and on. I climbed up the corporate ladder. I was with many famous people. On our record company rosters were Bruce Springsteen, Michael Jackson, Billy Joel, Barbra Streisand, and on and on. It was the biggest record company in the world, by far. At one point we were making $450,000,000 pretax profits for the year. That's more than all of what MCA made that year. But I was still crazy.

I would challenge Lew Wasserman, the head of MCA. I did terrible things to him. He wouldn't have arguments with me in public, but I had no problem starting fights with him. I didn't care—it was consistent with my image.

So this went on. My drinking had escalated,, and I was getting sicker and sicker, on all levels. Emotionally, spiritually, and physically for sure. Finally, in 1989 my friendly doctor, who had been tracking my health, told me, "You have three months to live. Your liver count is over the moon." He then described one of the forms of alcoholic death, which is cirrhosis. He described a lady who died from this disease: "Her legs shriveled up, her arms shriveled up, her stomach was distended, and her system backed up until she vomited her own feces." That's where I was headed.

Being who I am, I waited it out for four months while deciding what to do. Then I decided to go to Hazelden, in Minnesota. I took the corporate plane, of course. It was a Falcon 900, a $40 million airplane. Aside from the pilot, I flew there with the company nurse because I was really scared. I got off the plane and they put me into a van with a bunch of other people, and I said, "What, are you crazy? Where's my limo?" On the way to Hazelden I saw a bar and asked the driver to stop so I could have my last drink, and he said, "You've had your last drink."

I was not a very good candidate to get sober because I thought I knew it all. So I went through the Hazelden program, and after about a year of sobriety, everything was going real well. My liver count had returned to normal. I forgot to mention, when I first got to Hazelden, they took a blood test, and I said to the nurse, "How am I doing?" And she didn't reply. I asked her again, "Am I going to be all right?" And she said, "I don't know." You don't expect to hear that from a medical person. You expect them to say, "Yeah, yeah, you're going to be fine."

So in a month my liver count was down to high-normal. My emotional, spiritual condition, however, has taken a long time to heal. People talk about a slow recovery and get upset with that, wanting a fast recovery instead. But people who do recover quickly, who snap right back and get better—then what? Some go out and drink again.

After a year, Sony and I had a parting of the ways and I was fired. I ended up with a ton of money, but I didn't know what to do. The structure of my life was gone. The power was gone. I asked somebody, "How long will my legend and patina live?" And they said, "Maybe a year."

It's nineteen years later and people call me all the time. They say, "Oh, Walter, we need you for an interview. We are doing the history of recorded music, and it can't be done without you."

But that kind of recognition doesn't matter that much to me anymore. Now, my life is completely different. I have, as I remarked earlier, enough money for me. I tried to resurrect my past life by starting new record companies and this and that, and I failed. Had I succeeded, I would probably be dead now, because I would have assumed a mantle of phony power, which could have led me back to my old habits and I might have died. I have a strong belief now that there is something up there, in the cosmic field. God, or whatever you want to call it, is taking care of me. My job is to allow it to happen and then do the right thing. I know it sounds corny, that my life has become a cliché, but my life is totally altered today.

So, anyway, my resentment against Sony is gone. I don't want to be in their shoes; I don't want to be in the music business. To me my recovery is more than not drinking and not drugging. I feel my soul has been cleansed to a large extent. Had I done a lot of bad stuff in my past? Yes, I was in a position of power and I abused it.

I now do a lot of service. I've gone back one generation. Instead of following my mother's dictates to always get ahead, no matter what, I'm now following my grandmother's dictates, and hers were at odds with her daughter's. My grandmother would always say, "What did you do for somebody else today?" And she was completely serious about it. And now I'm doing the same thing. Am I her? No! First of all I don't look like her! But I am turning a little bit into her. I've heard people say, "I'm turning into the man I always wanted to be." This? This is wimpy. I'm from the Leo Durocher era. "Nice guys finish last," Leo, the manager of the Brooklyn Dodgers, always said. That may be, but now I'm not playing the same game.

I do a great deal of service today. I'd say half my life is about doing service. I do this thing out in New Jersey called Eva's Village. This shelter, named after a nun, serves seven thousand meals a day to indigents. Their attitude is, "What can we do to help these people?" Not, "How much money can we make?" I spend a lot of time with them. I bring recovery meetings into the shelter. I'm involved with some people who are opening a recovery center. I'm involved with a lot of people. I found that I have a creative side I didn't know about. I thought I was an administrator. I'm on the board of a couple of companies.

My life is really wilder than my wildest dreams, but the biggest thing about it is that I don't wake up in terror. I have bad dreams, we all do, but now I wake up and think to myself, "I wonder what the Force has in mind for me today?" If I just let it, the Force can do a much better job of running things than I can. And, I don't live in terror.

# 15

# Marv Seppala

*A moment's insight is sometimes worth a life's experience.*

—O. W. HOLMES, *THE PROFESSOR AT THE BREAKFAST TABLE*

Marv Seppala was born in Seattle and as a child lived in two big cities, San Jose, California, and Minneapolis, but his family settled in southern Minnesota before he entered sixth grade. It was in this rural, pastoral setting that he got on the wrong track during his teens.

Dr. Seppala's personal history is closely tied to that of the Hazelden Foundation, where he was one of the first adolescents to be treated for addiction, in the mid-1970s. Following treatment, he developed an interest in medicine, worked in a lab at the Mayo Clinic, and went on to earn a medical degree. He has been clean and sober since September 1975. He was seventeen when he entered treatment at Hazelden and nineteen when he got sober.

In 1984 Dr. Seppala graduated from the Mayo Medical School in Rochester, Minnesota, completing his residency in psychiatry at the University of Minnesota Hospital. He left a successful private practice to become the chief medical director at Hazelden. There he had responsibility for medical care throughout Hazelden's facilities nationwide, and his record of accomplishments included championing a physicians-in-residence training program and overseeing special recovery programs for addicted health care professionals, as well as promoting state-of-the-art addiction medical practices. He is at present medical director–CEO of Beyond Addictions in Portland, Oregon.

Marv and his wife, Linda, married at twenty. "It was a mistake except it worked out." With their son and daughter grown, college educated, and engaged in their own individual lives, the parents enjoy the Oregon outdoors, especially camping and backpacking several times a month in the Mount Hood area. A medical school buddy got him into skiing; Marv is an active skier and has taken a ski vacation with the same group of four physicians and a car mechanic every year of the last twenty.

His other passion is "trying to figure out new ways to help people. That's the piece I'm after—to help the most number of people possible. My bias was there was only one way to get sober and I promote the twelve steps, but I take a more objective look now and seek alternatives, as well."

Dr. Seppala had been advised not to mention his addiction when he applied to medical school, or they'd eliminate him for sure. After six months he told the dean he was in recovery from addiction, and the dean, a "great big friendly guy," was dumbfounded, absolutely silent. It ended their relationship.

In spring 2005 the quarterly alumni magazine of the Mayo Clinic ran a feature about Dr. Seppala, which started with his addiction and working in their lab. "From not being able to mention addiction to this, I think that's progress."

---

# MARV SEPPALA

I was born in Seattle. My mother and father, who are both Finnish, met in Tacoma, Washington, where there's a large Finnish community. They both spoke Finnish, but they didn't teach it to me because we lived next door to a University of Washington English professor who told them it would just confuse me if they taught me both languages. It was the 1950s and immigration meant being a part of a new culture, which also influenced their decision.

I had three younger brothers and a sister, and we all moved to San Jose, California, when I was very young. We lived there for four years and then moved to Bloomington, Minnesota, where we lived another four years before settling in Stewartville, Minnesota.

My parents seldom drank, not much at all. I never recall seeing them intoxicated. At around age twelve I was with some friends out on a farm. We had cleaned out the barn and the parents were gone for the evening so we stole some whiskey and drank it. It really struck me how wonderful I felt. I just really enjoyed that feeling of intoxication. The one thing I got out of it was that I knew I was going to do it again.

It took a while before I had another opportunity, because at that age it wasn't so easy getting alcohol, but ultimately we found more. In my early using days, starting so young, I didn't understand that people had to pay for liquor. So stealing it became the way to do it. There were no other options.

It's funny, but there wasn't really peer pressure on me to keep drinking. I was the one who was applying the peer pressure! I wanted to drink, but there weren't any other kids that wanted to do it with me. So I found new friends who wanted to and soon enough, around the age of fourteen, also found people who did drugs.

I had a friend whose older brother went off to college. I really looked up to this guy. He was on the high school varsity basketball team and a really good student. He even made the dean's list. An all-around amazing guy. I knew him through our church. He came back after his freshman year in college and asked my friend and me if we wanted to smoke some pot. I remember thinking, "I would never do that." This was unbelievable to me. In the sixties it wasn't so unusual, but it was my first exposure to it.

It just took me one week to get past the initial concerns I had about it. And, of course, I liked it and started smoking it as often as I could. And then amphetamines came along and I enjoyed those even more. In our small town there wasn't a drug dealer or anything. Just some people who used and sold to each other. It was kind of a friendly thing to do. Just a group of people who provided for each other when they could get something. It was pretty easy to find, and I just kept increasing my use of the stuff.

I was a sophomore in high school and I was using pretty much every weekend. At least drinking and smoking pot. I was also on the varsity basketball team, which was a big deal for me. Our first game was coming up on Tuesday, but that Saturday night, prior to the game, I went out with a friend and we had been drinking. He was driving and we were out in the country on a gravel road, and he rolled the car in a ditch. We had come to a T in the road, which he didn't see. I broke my collarbone and couldn't play in the game on Tuesday night. So instead of going to watch the game, I went out and got drunk and that was the first time I ever drank on a weekday. It was a revelation to me. "I can feel this good every day of the week."

That was an amazing discovery. So the frequency now became every day. Alcohol and pot and whatever other drug was around. I went downhill fast. I was using drugs or alcohol every day by the time I was fifteen, and I dropped out of school at seventeen as a senior in high school.

That was when my family took me by the collar and put me into rehab at Hazelden. Five years later, I learned that I was the first adolescent admitted at Hazelden for addiction treatment. It cleaned me up, but when it was over I didn't continue my follow-up care and began using again. They gave me a blank diploma at the high school graduation ceremony, and I spent the next summer struggling through a string of jobs, skipping work sometimes and moving on to the next job. My parents had had enough and threw me out of their house. I was living out of my car when I applied for a janitor's position at the Mayo Clinic. I lied on my application, saying I had graduated from high school. A couple of weeks later, Mayo called my parents, trying to track me down for an interview. Instead of a janitorial position, I was interviewing for a technician's job in a cardiovascular laboratory.

I really believe my higher power said this is where I belong and just plunked me down in this lab so I could be dramatically influenced the way I was there.

Working at the Mayo Clinic, in the hierarchy of a lab, I was at the bottom of the chart. But there was a spirit of mutual respect in the laboratory, and that meant I was included in many activities, including the Monday morning lab meetings where people could convey their information and presentations for meetings. So they would be asking me for my input. I saw myself as just a drug addict and was stricken with shame about myself. And here they were asking me. Dr. Donald, the head of the lab, would sometimes finish his presentation and ask me first if I had any questions.

Inspired by my work at the lab, I started to see my teachers again, in their homes, and ultimately finished all my work and got my high school diploma. This was a remarkable gift.

On my high school record it showed that during my senior year I missed two weeks of school. I actually missed about four months. So this was another gift. Later on, when I applied to college, that was the transcript they got. There was no evidence that I had all these problems—that I had dropped out and missed several months.

Back at the Mayo Clinic, I did something completely unusual, which I still don't understand. I didn't get along with my father well at all, but I called him and said, "I'm a mess; I'm using drugs and alcohol again. I'm scared I'm going to lose my job, and I need some help." So he said he'd come up and talk with me.

After my parents kicked me out of the house and disowned me, my father got involved with a place called Sunrise in Rochester, Minnesota. He helped get it off the ground. It was a place that kids with drug problems could go to and talk with folks. So he suggested that I go down there, and I said, "Well, maybe tomorrow." I was trying to put it off, but he insisted, so we ended up going there and we talked with a counselor. Somehow I got caught up in this, and so I went back there again, and they had a group going. Since I had been through treatment already, I knew more about addiction than they did. They were pretty green. After a couple of weeks, one day I told the group that when I was in treatment they told me I needed to go to twelve-step meetings, and that's what I was going to do, because it wasn't going to help me being here. So I quit going and found a twelve-step meeting.

On a Sunday morning, in Rochester, Minnesota, I walked in and there were only three guys there, and they were all over seventy. And that was the meeting. It was wonderful, and bizarre at the same time. I didn't mind that they were all old. I was very shy and pretty scared about doing this and had never been to a meeting, and these guys didn't expect me to talk, and I didn't. Afterwards they said, "Why don't you come back next week?"

So the next week I went back, and I kept going. Every Sunday morning. The meeting actually grew. More people were attending every week. Over the next six months, all three of these guys died. At the time it didn't faze me, even though these guys had saved my life. I was so self-centered. I actually stayed clean and sober the whole six months, yet it didn't occur to me that their deaths might have some effect on me. I was going to those meetings because these guys asked me to.

I eventually started talking. For the first six months I didn't say anything. I didn't do anything. I didn't work the steps. I didn't get a sponsor. But I was doing as good as I had in my entire life. I was feeling so good that I thought I really didn't need those meetings. Life was going so well. It was unbelievable. So, this one Sunday, I missed the meeting, and on Monday, the very next day I grabbed some cocaine out of a cabinet at work and did it. It was like an automatic response. It was unplanned, but there I was sitting in the bathroom snorting cocaine.

I walked back to the lab and decided to call this guy I'd been meaning to ask to be my sponsor. I hadn't had the courage to do so, but I called him. I said, "John, I'd really like to talk to you," and John, who worked two blocks away, said, "Come on over." I said, "I can't come until after work," which was not true. I wanted to do as much of that cocaine as possible. And I did. Probably more than I did in my life, and I didn't even get high. All I got was unbelievable pain after finally getting a taste of recovery, six months' worth, and then losing it. The whole pain of my addiction was back, and the hopelessness was even worse. Because the only thing anyone had ever told me that would work and help me to stay sober was these twelve-step meetings, and now they didn't work either. So I honestly thought I was hopeless and that I would never stop. That this was my fate.

So I go over to see John, with all this in my head, and he had to leave to go coach his son's pee-wee football team. He said, "You can come with me, and we'll talk afterwards." So I'm sitting on the sidelines watching him coach and thinking how messed up my life is. Afterwards we went over to his house and started talking. I told him, "I've been to treatment. I've tried to quit on my own. Now I've tried twelve-step meetings and that doesn't work either." And John said, "It works just fine, but you haven't started yet, and this is what I'd like you to do. . . ." He suggested I work the steps with him, that I do a tenth-step inventory to review my day, and do it every day. That I start talking at the meetings and that I read the program's literature.

I was so scared that if I didn't do this stuff exactly as he told me to, I'd go back to using. So for the first time in my life I did what I was told. I just believed what John was telling me. He'd been sober for some time. Maybe five or six years. That seemed like forever to me. And so I did it. I did an inventory every night for five years, because I was so scared that if I didn't do it, I might use again.

I've been sober since that day, in September 1975. I stayed at my job in the lab. The heads of the lab, Drs. David Donald and John Shepherd, were world-famous researchers, and physicians from all over the world came to work under them. So I had the chance to meet these amazing doctors of varied backgrounds, who'd come to our lab and stay for a year or so. They would often ask me what I was going to do with my life, and I had no answer for them. I didn't know. It hadn't crossed my mind. Then one day I got this manila interclinic envelope. It bore the name and the department on it, and it had "Dr. Marvin Seppala" written on it. And I kept thinking about that; I still have it.

Shortly after, I started thinking, "I really like what these guys do. I think I want to be a doctor." So I went to my sponsor, John, and told him, "I want to go to college because I want to be a doctor," and if he were to have doubts in any way, I probably would have crumbled. I had no self-confidence. And fortunately John said, "You know, Marv, if it's God's will, it will happen." And I hung on to that.

I was really naive about how to go to college. I didn't seek help from anybody. The guys in the lab offered help, but I didn't take them up on it. I only applied to one college. I told myself that if I got in, great, but if I didn't, that would be God's will and it would be fine—I wouldn't go to college. That was my thinking, instead of, "I'll apply to five schools, and maybe I'll get into one of them."

St. Olaf College in Northfield, Minnesota, was known for its pre-med program; it's a really good small liberal arts college. And that's where I applied. This was the test for me: if it's God's will, I'm going; and if it's not, that's the way it goes. And I get in and my high school record shows that I just missed a couple of weeks and that I had good grades. So I start college on my first-year anniversary in recovery. And I go from there.

The whole time in college, I wanted to become a doctor. It was extremely difficult that first year, because I had ruined my memory and learning to use it again was difficult. But by the end of the first semester, it started to come round. My memory was definitely improving.

The following summer, I married my wife, Linda. We had known each other since eighth grade in Stewartville. Her family had moved away but we had exchanged addresses and wrote each other letters through high school. She visited me while I was in treatment, always had faith in me, and after her high school graduation we started dating. We were twenty years old, I was barely sober, and somehow we're still together. We married at an early age, for all the wrong reasons, and everything was stacked against us. But we have a great relationship.

When I had been sober for five years, I got into medical school, at Mayo. I really wanted to go there. I had worked there every summer during college and was really familiar with the place. I was kind of worried about medical school and my sobriety, knowing it would be a real challenging time. Would I be able to do my disciplines to stay sober—going to meetings and the like? But that worked out just fine.

Interesting things happened. I started medical school thinking I was going to be a surgeon, like a lot of the guys I had worked with in the lab. That was my goal. Two years into medical school I saw how little attention was paid to addiction. Doctors don't care about it, don't research it, don't do anything about it. I was complaining about this all the time. Finally, two cardiologists that attended the recovery meetings took me aside and said, "Marv, you've got to quit bitching about this and do something about it." This conversation opened my mind to another possibility besides surgery, and I thought, "Maybe I can go to work in the area of addiction." I looked around and realized the best way would be to go into psychiatry and specialize in addiction. And that's what I did. I applied for psychiatric programs on the East and West Coasts because I didn't want to stay in Minnesota. I didn't have enough money to visit both coasts and do the interviews, so I didn't know what I should do. I started a process of praying about it. My prayer to God was, "I need some direction or more money." All of a sudden I started getting rejection letters from every West Coast program I applied to and acceptance letters from every East Coast program. So it became really clear. I went to the East Coast and looked at all these programs, and none of them had anything decent going on about addiction.

So I returned to Mayo, and I'm walking through the administration building one day, and a secretary came up to me and said, "Marv, the University of Minnesota called and said you need to complete your application if you want to interview for a residency here." I said, "I didn't apply there." But then I thought, "What the heck?" So I sent in an application and went for an interview. I was driving up the highway to Minneapolis, and on the way I'm suddenly struck with the idea that this is the right place. This is where I belong, the University of Minnesota. Then I get scared. How am I going to perform in this interview?

Finally, I arrive and park my car in a lot overlooking the Mississippi River and I'm staring at this river, and suddenly I realize that if this is where I belong, I *can't* screw up the interview. As I'm thinking this, an eagle flew by, in downtown Minneapolis! So I settled down knowing this is going to be fine.

My interview went extremely well, and I was accepted there. Not only did they have a psychiatry department, but they had a fellowship in addiction and a real emphasis on addiction throughout the program. It was ideal for me. I also knew a couple of people in recovery there and attended meetings with them. I was able to continue my program despite the rigors of residency training. I was at the hospital every other night for a year or two. It was pretty tough to do the work and stay focused on my recovery, but it worked out well.

At the end of my training I moved to Portland, Oregon, where there was a job available working in a dual diagnosis program with people who had both addiction and psychiatric problems, which I'd been trained to do. I started to learn every aspect of helping people with addictions. I was pretty biased toward the twelve-step programs from my own addiction, almost to the point of believing that was the only way. Thank goodness I learned that there are other alternative treatments. As a physician you have to determine what's good for people who come to see you. For most people the twelve steps are probably the best way—but they're not for everybody. There are many things besides the twelve-step programs that can enhance recovery, and I learned about those as well. I had some great teachers throughout my life, both in and out of my training, and the fellowship of my twelve-step program. One reason I still go to meetings is that I feel a strong obligation to help others, just as I was helped. I also don't want to risk going back to where I was. I've been sober a long time and I know I have something to offer to those who are new. Being of service is one of the greatest gifts of recovery. The cliché is that you have to give it (sobriety) away to keep it, but in my experience that is absolutely true.

So, I worked in this dual-diagnosis program and had a private practice. Eventually, I moved back to Minnesota because a job had come up at the Hazelden adolescent program. They needed a psychiatrist. I had always wanted to work there, so I did that for a period of time, but I didn't advance, and we just loved it in the Northwest, so we moved back. Shortly after the move, Hazelden wanted to hire me as national medical director. However, I only stayed there for nine months; it just wasn't right for me. So we returned to Oregon, where I got involved with a treatment center called Springbrook NW, outside of Portland. Shortly thereafter, Hazelden purchased Springbrook NW, so there I go again. Hazelden brought me back as chief medical officer of the whole organization, but I could stay here in Oregon. I did that for almost five years. It was absolutely remarkable to be able to work at that level in a program that I had been in as a high school dropout. I had sort of come full circle. Along the way I had a chance to write a couple of books: a book for clinicians about the twelve steps and, more recently, I teamed with a pain expert at the Mayo Clinic and we wrote *Pain-Free Living for Drug-Free People*. It's a guideline on how to make good decisions if you have to have treatment for pain while in recovery—making good decisions and recognizing the risks involved.

My life is unbelievable. I left Hazelden because they wanted me to move back to Minnesota, and I didn't want to leave Oregon. My kids were just starting college and we wanted to stay on the West Coast. I left Hazelden and started an outpatient addiction program here in Portland, where we also do detoxification in people's homes for alcoholism. We place certified nurses' aides in the homes and provide detoxification services and then get them involved in outpatient treatment. It's been really an exciting time for me. I've opened a private practice treating people with addictions who also have other psychiatric issues that need to be addressed. It's been fun because when I was at Hazelden for those five years, I was an administrator and seldom had direct contact with people who needed help, but that is where my heart is. I prefer a balance of many activities at work.

I have two wonderful children. My wife and I are still married, after thirty years, which is amazing in itself. We've gone through a lot together. One of my biggest fears was that one of my children would have an addiction problem, given their genetics. I've told them all about addictions since they were very young. Of course, they're not out of the woods yet, but it appears that neither one of them has a problem at this point.

I've been sober over thirty-two years and my children are in their early twenties, so they've never seen me use. They've both heard stories and I told them my story. I wanted them to know what it was like. I've been sober a long time, and I still go to recovery meetings. Early on I found that sobriety by itself was not enough; that I had to live my life based on spiritual principles associated with the twelve steps. Because I did that I really had the opportunity to change and grow and lead a life I could be proud of. My daily goal is to live the best life I can, to express love, and to be of service.

# 16

# Bob Goodale

*We must uncenter our minds from ourselves;*
*We must unhumanize our views a little,*
*    and become confident*
*As the rock and ocean we were made from.*

—ROBINSON JEFFERS, "CARMEL POINT"

B ob Goodale, a rugged, all-American Midwesterner, is the sort of person you'd like to have on your team—most any team. He plays fair, exhibits quick thinking, and is skillful, realistic, and full of energy and mirth. He is a recovering alcoholic with a delightfully outrageous and irrepressible spirit. For instance, once (long after he gave up drinking) Bob danced topless in a hula skirt on the busiest corner in downtown Charlotte, North Carolina, kitty-corner to the Bank of America headquarters to pay off a bet. (His performance ended up in a three-column photo on page one of the *Charlotte Observer*.)

Bob was CEO of three food-processing and distribution companies before becoming president of Harris Teeter, a major supermarket chain in the Carolinas and Virginia. During his tenure at Harris Teeter, revenue doubled, operating income tripled, and the number of stores increased from 75 to 125.

From 1993 to 1997 he served as North Carolina deputy secretary of commerce. When his job for the state ended, Bob went to work for the Institute at Biltmore, developing strategies for nonprofits and communities to increase their capacity for service. "Fascinating work with organizations that fight PETA, booze and drugs, homophobia and other prejudices, and the digital divide, among others."

Specific projects under his management in his second, volunteer career have included strategic plans for North Carolina Partnership for Children, Forsyth Early Childhood Partnership, and the Knowledge Center in Western North Carolina. He was project manager for the creation of the Western North Carolina Center for Technology Commercialization, funded by UT-Battelle and Oak Ridge National Laboratory. His latest project is to develop a plan for a citizen soldier support program, funded by a Congressional appropriation to University of North Carolina-Chapel Hill.

Bob has a B.S. from Iowa State University and an MBA from the University of Kansas. He lives in several states, and he and his wife have six children—three he adopted with his first wife, two hers, and one, to quote Bob, "homemade," and eleven grandchildren.

A very present-oriented happy man, Bob sums up his work life today as follows: "I'm not someone to retire. My workshop is my office." After a pause he adds, "Let me know if you have any work for me. I can still clean wallpaper and windows, strap cans, and dice onions, and I remain a certified sauerkraut runner."

---

# BOB GOODALE

My ancestor on my father's side was a seventeenth-century brewmaster in Suffolk, England, so I have an ancestral link to the ale business and alcoholism. My mother was an alcoholic, and who knows the lineage in back of that; I know I have an abundance of genetic predisposition to alcoholism.

When we graduated from high school, five of my best friends and I went to Clear Lake, Iowa, where we spent the night camping out. We found some beer, of which I drank a six-pack, and while I recalled the next day how I felt when I drank the beer, I didn't recall what I was doing when I went to bed. That was the first of thousands of mornings when I woke up not knowing what I was doing when I "fell asleep." I was soon to be an eighteen-year-old, and that was it.

I graduated from Iowa State University with respectable grades and considerable honors, all the time continuing not to know what I was doing when I went to bed. Blackouts—they were expected; I thought they happened to everybody. I loved what alcohol did for me, so my drinking continued unabated. I got a series of good jobs and would continue to fall up the ladder of success, but, of course, my dependency on alcohol increased. I got to the place where I was hiding it, making sure that I had plenty of drink—supply was extremely important. I couldn't even go to a movie for fear of being away from booze for three hours.

It got to where I drank in the morning, stretching my orange juice. Finally, I didn't need the orange juice. And meanwhile I had married, had had three children, and was thirty-eight years old.

I was morally, spiritually bankrupt. I had an intact family and still held a job, but my life was awful. I said to myself that I had two big problems: I couldn't drink like everyone else, and my marriage was in disarray. So rather than go to talk to a parish priest or minister, in my grandiosity I went to consult with the bishop. And so, in 1971, over three martinis apiece, the bishop and I agreed we'd work on the marriage first. I contacted him again about six months later, after an appalling February night culminating in me passing out, running my car off the road into a stubble field outside

Omaha, and setting the stubble field on fire from the sparks from my car. When I came to from my blackout, flames surrounded my car. That's all I remember. Hell still comes to mind. I had to call the fire department the next morning to ask if what I thought had happened actually did. It did!

So I phoned the bishop, and he recommended I go to a treatment center in Omaha that had just opened. I was their client number seven, the bishop was number forty-six.

I didn't want to go but couldn't deny that my life had become chaotic and unmanageable. I was barely functioning professionally, and I was just right next to the world's worst parent and husband—you name it! It's still unimaginable to me that with very few exceptions I have no memory of holding my infant and toddler children. Zero! Thankfully, a few years ago my children gave me an album with pictures of me holding them and being with them. It remains impossible to talk about that today, forty-five years later, without tears. But it is important to remember, to talk about it.

I was certainly sick, but what really saddened me is I was bad. I was almost overpowered by guilt and shame when I stopped drinking, and when I walked into that treatment center, and someone told me they were powerless over alcohol, I said to myself, "That's the answer, that's it!" That was one of those aha moments. So that's what the deal was. For nineteen years, doctors would ask at annual physicals, "How much do you drink?" And I'd lie and seriously understate the quantity and frequency. But one doctor told me I should cut back on even that quantity and frequency— the same doctor that was treating me for hypertension with blood thinners and the like. About four months before I stopped drinking, I was in the hospital because I was bleeding from about every orifice. I had esophageal bleeding. There was just blood everywhere. Nobody talked to me about my drinking. Yet the moment I walked into the treatment center, there my diagnosis was: powerless over alcohol. I knew that—I had said to the bishop, "I can't drink like everybody else," and he never suggested I should seek some help on that—no, we worked on the marriage.

Anyway, I got where I needed to be, and that was the important thing. And that began my journey back. After leaving the facility, I found myself divorced and remarried, and there was a swamp of fear, guilt, and shame to be drained. I do give myself high marks for being a part-time parent and will furthermore say I'm a damn good parent of my adult children, as well as a responsible, loving grandfather, but I was not there the way I should have been with my adolescent children.

Except for a couple of times, since 1972 I've never felt a desire to drink. Every once in a while when I see a commercial or movie where someone has a gin and tonic or a martini, my mouth waters, but these times haven't been an overpowering kind of thing. I don't desire to drink, but the reflex is there—amazing, to me.

The chaos drinking caused had ended, and now I had to deal with its consequences. What faced me was learning to be an adult, make mature decisions, and live a sober life. Abstinence is one level of recovery, but sobriety is another; sobriety has to do with more than just not drinking. It has to do with spirituality, trusting your higher power, which I chose to call God. It has to do with "cleaning house," by which I mean cleaning your soul, heart, and mind. And it has to do with helping others. That's the foundation. If I don't drink but do trust my higher power, "clean my house," and help others, then I'm sober. When I just don't drink, then I'm abstinent but hardly sober!

That was a process for me and continues to be a process today. I was thirty-eight when I stopped drinking. I call the 1960s the decade I missed. I was on another planet. For example, here's how I responded towards JFK's assassination. That day, November 22, 1963, I was having lunch with my boss, and he mentioned Kennedy was going to be in Dallas, and I said, "I hope they shoot the son of a bitch." Can you believe that? That's what I was—put bluntly, the drinking had suppressed my scruples. As always, I've got tears now thinking of it.

Professionally, I was welcomed back from treatment. To me, it was like, "Well, let's see what happens." By the way, when I went back to that company after being in treatment, I absolutely did penance—not that I had stolen from them, but in reality I did steal from them: I didn't give them my mind, my capacity to do things that I could do. It was really a living amends that I gave to that company for five years, and I did it well.

Physically, there were a lot of changes, too. I had been born with a clubfoot. It had been straightened with casts and braces when I was a toddler but had become increasingly arthritic. I couldn't walk three blocks without a lot of pain, which was a good excuse to stretch my orange juice in the morning with vodka. After I stopped drinking, Jan made an appointment with an orthopedic surgeon. He asked me to take off my sock, took a look at it, and said, "I can fix that." But he did more than fix my foot; by example of his care for kids and others, he showed me what I needed to be—he began the process of fixing my heart and soul. After the operation, one of my kids gave me a needlepoint kit, so I started doing needlepoint and did needlework obsessively. I rationalized that the needlepoint was like working a recovery program—not like a day at a time exactly, but a stitch at a time! If I made a mistake, I said it would be throwing the whole piece away, like throwing away recovery. But since throwing away recovery wasn't an option, I'd fix my needlework mistake and proceed on, a stitch at a time.

I was counting my production, how many stitches I did an hour, and I figured out I was doing needlepoint forty hours a week. I wasn't going to any meetings—I was doing needlepoint. In fact, that's how I knew that I had time to go to graduate school! I was abstinent, but all that time I was not paying attention to sobriety.

I was driven to make up for the lost decade professionally. I knew I had a big flat side that I had to get fixed. My B.S. degree was in dairy science, but my profession was food sales and marketing, and while I could read operating statements, I didn't know a debit from a credit and bluffed my way around anything dealing with finance. In 1977 we were living in a suburb of Chicago, where the company had moved. On a flight to see a customer, I glanced at the *Wall Street Journal* the passenger in front of me was reading. An ad for the M.B.A. program at the University of Chicago caught my eye. When I changed planes, I bought a copy of the *Journal* and decided at once to discuss it with my boss. The next day I discussed the opportunity with him; he was supportive and said he'd discuss it with his boss, the CEO. A few days later, my boss told me the CEO had turned down my request, not because of the price, which I thought was outrageous, but he didn't want me to have alternate Fridays off to go to class. So it was clear to me that I had to move on. I was ready for a change.

Within days I mentioned to one of my customers that I would make a change if the right thing came about, and he said, "We've been wanting for you to say that." So I went to work for the then-largest food wholesaler in the world, which didn't have anyone experienced in dairy department procurement and merchandising, which was my long suit. I took the job for a little less money than I was making, but I knew the company and the individuals I'd be working with and felt the sky was the limit. We moved to Lawrence, Kansas, near company headquarters. A few weeks into my new job, I told my boss, who remains a good friend today, that I wanted to go to the University of Kansas for an M.B.A. He said, "Great, go for it." I said, "But I want to go full time." He said, "I told you to go for it!" And so I did.

I was yet to learn the difference between abstinence and sobriety, which means a great deal to me today. How's this, for instance? I went to school full time, and had a full-time job, with considerable travel involved. And I traveled and did all of the attendant stuff. Yet I was self-involved—selfish, really—looking after myself and *what I needed to do to get where I wanted*, but missing a key piece of progress in my life. I was a part-time husband and a part-time father to my now six children—my wife Jan's three children in Lawrence and my three in Omaha two hundred miles away, whom I saw every other weekend.

So I got my M.B.A. in the prescribed two years and then more or less went to the company boss again and said, "Now what?" He told me I was doing great—and I was, because at work I leveraged my experience and knowledge and focused, focused, focused on doing only the critical success factors. And the boss actually said, "We're concerned you're going to burn out." The clock was continuing to tick; I'd missed a decade. I was fired up and ready for me.

So I began contacting a few people to let them know I'd make a change if the right thing came along. A few weeks passed, and I called a long-time friend who said, "The right thing came yesterday!" He said he had to find it, as he'd thrown the job notice away. Fortunately, he found it, and six or eight weeks later I was the white blackbird, the needle in the haystack for a terrific job, the number-two job at a large supermarket chain. They offered it saying if everything went well, and it did, I would eventually become the CEO.

A couple of years passed—the job was going well; I remained abstinent but also in a constant state of vague, uneasy aggravation about myself. For one thing, I was very uncomfortable that I hadn't told the individuals who had hired me that I was in recovery. Anyone that knew me in my previous jobs knew I had stopped drinking and why, but I intentionally withheld that information in the interviews, fearing it would jeopardize my chances. So, one day, I told my immediate boss, the CEO, that I was a recovering alcoholic and that I wanted to go downtown to meet with the chairman of the board to let him know I was in recovery. The CEO reluctantly agreed; a few days later we met with the COB. I told him I was a recovering alcoholic, to which he replied, "We knew that when we hired you." What a gift of freedom the COB gave me! From that day on, everyone who I worked for or with or who worked for me would know sooner rather than later that I was a recovering alcoholic. That was twenty-five years ago.

Now when I advocated for effective EAP programs, I could talk about my personal experience and it made a difference. I remember participating in an intervention for an associate. To our surprise, the professional who led the intervention urged the associate's spouse to bring their five-year-old daughter to the session. So there we were in the circle, each telling the associate how the consequences of his drinking made us feel: angry, disappointed, hurt. Then the professional told the associate that arrangements had been made for him to immediately go to treatment and asked, "Will you go?" All of us except the five-year-old knew to keep quiet until the associate spoke. The long silence was broken by the tiny voice coming from the child on her mother's lap, saying, "Daddy, please go!" There wasn't a dry eye in the room as he left for treatment.

About the same time I let my associates know I was a recovering alcoholic, I was trying to get in better physical shape, so Jan made an appointment for me to talk to the local YMCA. So I got into exercise—excessive and obsessive exercise, yet another example of achieving abstinence but not sobriety. Normal people would exercise three or four times a week, whereas my routine was to go in the morning and go again at night. Keeping my endorphins high, all that tripe!

Here's my take on that. I would leave work in my business uniform, a coat and tie, at, say, 5:30, because my favorite group at the YMCA was at six o'clock, and that was twenty minutes away on the busiest street in the city. So I left in my business suit and arrived in my shorts, T-shirt, and gym shoes, which means a fair portion of the time I was going bare-assed down the busiest street in the twenty-fifth largest city in the U.S.

Is this sane? Is this sober? Of course not! But, you know, meanwhile I've still got all these familial responsibilities of kids and all that, and I was not dealing with those issues that relate to my moral center. My definition of success had been money, and it seemed to me that every time I got more of those commodities, it never fixed me.

I remember the day I learned that I was going to be president of that company. I'd connived and worked for years for that kind of a job. But that day, when there was a reason to celebrate, was one of the worst days of my life, *because it didn't fix me*. I had become a needlework expert, had received an M.B.A., was a fitness freak, had gone to therapy, and had achieved my goal of becoming a CEO. And I was miserable.

I was torn with the conflicts of wanting to be a whole person, a better husband, a better father, while working too many hours to satisfy the demands of the business and the community. Because I was being more than a bit of an adrenaline junkie, I thrived on pressure, still chasing the decade that I'd missed. I hadn't given any priority to self-discovery. My life has been a series of finding out what doesn't work in order to find out what does work. I was miserable. I knew what didn't work, which included drinking; and I had enough sense to know I'd better do something else. I'd learned about dry drunks, and it finally occurred to me that I'd been on a decade-long dry drunk, and I'd better do something about it.

I could talk the language of recovery, and I'd been abstinent for over ten years. I remembered the card in the treatment center near the coffee and apples that read "I'm confused because I give such good advice but set such a bad example." That's me in spades, I thought. And that's when I started a journey to become sober, to understand that it wasn't about drying out but about working a program of recovery; don't drink, trust God, clean house, and help others.

I loved reading about Ed Carlson, who became president of United Airlines in the 1970s after parachuting in from Western International Hotels, and I felt like what I was reading about him. Like me, he didn't feel connected with his associates either—he formed the NETMA (Nobody Ever Tells Me Anything) Society at UAL and decided to do Q&A sessions. He'd get everyone who could come to the sessions and ask them to bring any questions or comments about United Airlines, and he would stand there and answer every one. And those he couldn't answer he'd get back to the person later. "Bingo!" I thought, "That's for me." For the next year I had about ten of those sessions and received over three thousand questions and comments and not one of them was written with a poison pen.

I remember the first Q&A session. Trust hadn't been established. At this and other sessions from five or six stores, we'd invite the grocer manager, the market manager, the head cashier, the produce manager, and the manager or comanager from each store—so there would be twenty-five to thirty associates there, and their questions and other people's would be in a big box. I'd read each question out loud and then answer it or tell the group I'd get back to them, which I did. At the first Q&A session, I read one comment that said, "Please do something about the toilet paper." I discovered the questions ran in patterns—a half-dozen more said the same thing. I wondered, "What's going on? What's the deal?" Here we were in upper management telling the employees how we loved our family, and that kind of malarkey, and what they really knew about us came from a buyer who in his zeal to keep costs down had bought the cheapest, most industrial-strength toilet paper for the store bathrooms! Someone in the group commented that it really didn't save any money because of the quantity it took to get the job done! And that's how they knew how the folks at headquarters really felt about them.

I called it the Tissue Issue. Clearly the problem wasn't just about the toilet tissue. The numerous comments got us thinking. If you go back to the early eighties, you'd see that the supermarket bathrooms were way in the back and often nasty, and to get to them you had to walk past all the pallets and boxes, and it was awful. Meanwhile, we were talking about our fine produce and fine meats—it didn't make sense. If you really wanted to demonstrate concern for employees and customers, you better start with the bathrooms.

So this for me was about being open to ideas, about listening to others. After deliberating, we put a million dollars into bathrooms. I joked that we couldn't justify this *ass*et on the *bottom* line. But the fact is I was on the road to sobriety; I was listening and being receptive to new ideas.

The real action was always in the stores, and as a result of that, I could go into a store and say to the manager, "How are things going?" and typically he'd say everything was fine. I'd say, "Are the trucks on time?" And he'd say, "No, the trucks are never on time." That would give me the opening to say, "I know they're never on time and we're working on it. What else is going on?" So we'd laugh and begin listening to each other.

Then I'd walk back to the meat department. "How's everything?" "Everything's fine." I'd say, "How are the short ribs?" "The short ribs are shit!" And I'd reply, "I know they're shit. We're working on it; we'll get it fixed. I need to know that, guys." And we'd laugh and begin listening to each other.

After a while I began to get terrific feedback. Then I had the idea that I'd take collect phone calls from anybody, including "Anonymous," and, you know, I averaged three or four a week for several years. Everybody had my phone number. I'd get calls at home from customers, too. We were a pretty large company, about 8,000 employees and 110 stores, so it was about being open. I am in sobriety; I always answer my phone. I don't want anyone in the middle, and when I speak of my recovery now, I don't want any barriers, including a lectern. God knows I've had enough barriers! I am far from perfect and will always be working on it. Don't drink, trust God, clean house, help others. . . .

All of this led to an invitation to serve on a Drugs in the Workplace panel that would report to President Reagan when he visited Duke University in February 1988. We were informed that we each had three minutes to speak to President Reagan at the convocation in Cameron Indoor Stadium, home of the Duke Blue Devils. That morning we met with Secretary of Labor Ann McLaughlin. "Trust God," I thought and tossed my prepared remarks, deciding to wing it.

Cameron Indoor Stadium was packed; people seemed to be hanging from the rafters! I was the last to speak; everyone else spoke from written text, and then it was my turn. I began, "Mr. President, my name is Bob Goodale, and I'm a recovering alcoholic. I know the hell of addiction and the God-given miracle of recovery." To my amazement, the place erupted in applause, which would happen again and again as I spoke. The students really got into it when I told the president that there were thousands of mornings that I woke up not knowing what I was doing when I went to bed!

But another amazing thing was happening. The president became teary eyed! The observer in me thought, "He's going to lose it," while the participant in me kept on talking. Then it was time to leave. The president ignored the governor and the chancellor and made a beeline for me. Shaking my hand, he whispered in my ear, "Thank you. My father found what you found a year before he died." Here was the president of the United States sharing his not-so-secret family secret! I wondered if he'd ever come to grips with his father's alcoholism, and if he had, what a different speech he would have delivered that day at Duke. But I also thought that if he had previously come to grips with his father's alcoholism, he might not have been president, because he didn't have to prove to his father that he was a success.

Serendipity struck again and I went to work side-by-side with a real turnaround artist. Two extremely high-net-worth individuals put together $20 million to go bottom-fishing for food companies and found, with my help, the world's largest carp. So my new-found friend and turnaround artist and I worked hundred-hour weeks for a year. The last time I spoke with one of the principals he said, "I don't know how the hell I could have $10 million in a year on this project."

At one of the companies where I worked, the CEO was a practicing alcoholic; several of his direct reports, including me, decided to talk privately to the chairman of the board about the CEO's inability to function because of his drinking and it was affecting his performance. I remember that of the five who raised the issue, several said they didn't sleep the night before. The board chair agreed there might be a problem; he knew someone who had known the CEO for a long time and arranged a meeting with the CEO's friend the next day. We later learned that when the CEO's friend greeted the board chair, he said, "I know why you're here." A week or so later, the chairman of the board asked the CEO to meet with him in the boardroom. When the CEO walked into the room, I'm told, and looked around at his friends from outside the company and from all over the country, he said, "What took you so long?"

For the past three years I'd been around all of this power and wealth. I didn't like what I observed—enslavement to *more, more, more*! Once again I was finding out what didn't work in order to find out what did work. It became increasing clear to me that success for me wasn't about power or money. It wasn't about what I did *for* a living, but what I did *with* my living. I decided I was going to do something meaningful with the second half of my adult life. I knew I didn't want to do what I'd done prior to that, not run companies or divisions. I decided to devote the second half of my adult life to the public sector. So I went to see a friend who was the CEO of a very large, successful utility who I'd previously worked with on a number of civic projects and told him, "I know what I don't want to do but haven't figured out what I want to do." He asked, "How much time do you have?" I said, "How much time do you need?" He said, "A large consulting firm has been hired by the city and county to look at the duplication of children's services. They need a loaned executive to show them around town—the typical thing. How about lending yourself?"

I want to be clear that I wasn't in any position to be a philanthropist! I'm rich in experience but the buck stops there. I was driving a ten-year-old car, just like I do today. I didn't drink, trusted God, was still cleaning house, and helped others.

It was a few weeks later when I saw the county manager, and explained I'd signed up and why. He said that Robert Wood Johnson had set up $50 million for $3 million grants to thirteen cities plus $10 million for evaluation to look for effective ways to reduce the demand for alcohol and drugs in at-risk communities with a population of about 125,000. Initially, about three hundred communities applied. RWJ awarded the greater part of the grant to eleven communities and held out the $3 million to two other communities if they could get their acts together. He said, "How about it, will you help us?" I said, "Absolutely."

That's how I learned about community development, because it was an at-risk neighborhood. And my African-American friends said to me with love, "Bob, we're tired of being told what to do by people who work in tall buildings, and wear coats and ties, and live in nice houses." So I began to learn about community development—again, how to listen, how to get work done.

The county got the grant, and serendipity struck again. I became the deputy secretary of commerce for North Carolina.

After doing that for four years, I went on to do strategic planning for nonprofits and communities. Sometimes I strayed from my commitment to devote the second half of my adult life to public service and became involved in several turnarounds and startups. I'm very passionate about my current assignment, to develop a plan to engage communities to support the resiliency of soldiers who have been deployed to Iraq and Afghanistan, as well as their families.

I approach life as a working person differently since sobriety. I have two photos in my office. In one, I'm shaking President Reagan's hand. In the other, I'm wearing a hula skirt. The real me is the one in the hula skirt.